ALEX KARADZIN

Kobe Bryant & The Mamba Mentality

Symphony of Greatness

Copyright © 2022 by Alex Karadzin

All rights reserved. No part of this publication may be reproduced, stored or transmitted in any form or by any means, electronic, mechanical, photocopying, recording, scanning, or otherwise without written permission from the publisher. It is illegal to copy this book, post it to a website, or distribute it by any other means without permission.

First edition

This book was professionally typeset on Reedsy.
Find out more at reedsy.com

Contents

Introduction	v
Kobe Bryant & The Mamba Mentality: Symphony of Greatness	vii
Kobe Bryant & The Mamba Mentality: The Symphony of Greatness Roadmap	x
1 Origin Story	1
The Rise of the Prodigy	6
The Decision That Forever Changed the Landscape of the NBA	14
2 The Power of Solitude & Introspection	20
Crossroads Moment: The Road to Retirement and The Journey into the Unknown	21
The Trait of The Great: Solitude as a Tool For Personal Development	29
Kobe's Spiritual Rituals for Peak Performance	37
3 Personal Mastery	39
Master at Work: The Performance that Cemented a Legacy	41
Mamba Mentality: The Simple Formula for Mastery	45
The Practice of a Master	49
Fundamentals: The Secret to Winning and Success	51
From Zero to Hero: The Genesis of The Mamba Mentality & The Essence of Mastery	54

4 The Identity & The Role of Alter-Ego	58
Recreate Yourself and Forge Your Greatest Destiny	64
The Black Mamba: The Character that Changed the Landscape of the Game	70
The Aftermath of a Dreadful Season: Kobe's Trial & Reputation, and The Evolution of Black Mamba Character	75
5 Uncompromising Integrity	78
The Clash of Opposing Ideologies: The Rise & Fall of the Most Dynamic Duo in the History of Sports	89
The Aftermath of the Crumble	98
6 Relentless Desire & Mental Warfare	103
Passing of The Torch	113
7 Evolution & Leadership	122
It's Always Darkest Before the Dawn: Personal Evolution & Compassionate Leadership	128
The Ultimate Leadership Test: Revenge Served With a Vengeance	135
8 Eternal Legacy: Greatness Echoes into Eternity	146
Give Back and Inspire the Next Generation	151
Beyond The Horizon: The Journey To Infinity	156
About the Author	161
Also by Alex Karadzin	165

Introduction

"It's the one thing you can control. You are responsible for how people remember you — or don't. So don't take it lightly.

If you do it right, your game will live on in others. You'll be imitated and emulated by those you played with, those you played against, and those who never saw you play at all.

So leave everything on the court. Leave the game better than you found it. And when it comes time for you to leave, leave a legend."

On January 26th, 2020, the world stood still. Humanity has just lost one of the Greats. Kobe Bryant, his daughter Gianna and seven others died in a helicopter accident.

Kobe Bryant was a universally beloved figure. His Greatness showed no boundaries when the entire planet united in grief. Kobe was a role model who inspired the whole world.

As a basketball player, without a shadow of a doubt, he is one of the Greatest ever to do it. His place in the pantheon of basketball Gods is unquestioned. Just like *Bill Russell, Karem Abdul Jabar, Magic, Larry Bird, and Michael Jordan,* **Kobe Bryant was a generational superstar.** One of the best players to ever grace the wooden court, Kobe Bryant, transcended the game of basketball.

However, in one regard, he is different from any other legend and stands alone.

Unlike all the others before him, Kobe's Greatness far exceeded the confines of the basketball court. He was a visionary entrepreneur, an author, a philanthropist, and a storyteller. In fact, he was so proficient at storytelling that after his 20-year NBA career with The Los Angeles Lakers, he told a story and won one of the most prestigious awards in the film industry.

He was just different than all the others. Kobe Bryant made Greatness look so effortless.

From the moment he emerged on the scene in high school, Kobe Bryant was a man driven by purpose. At the same time, he was guided by his curiosity, love for the game, and desire to win. His remarkable character and unique mindset are reflected in the way he played the game. On the basketball court, Kobe Bryant achieved everything he ever dreamed of. In his pursuit of Greatness, he raised the bar of excellence for future generations to exceed.

It wasn't just what he did on the court but how he did it. Kobe

Bryant was renowned as a fearless competitor who immortalized the mindset of winning and success.

Before he was taken from us, seemingly too soon, Kobe left his greatest gift to humanity. To those willing to embark on the journey of Greatness, Kobe Bryant left us with the *Roadmap to Greatness.*

His eternal legacy is The Mentality of Winning and Success, which is deeply intertwined with Kobe's approach to basketball, but also his way of life.

Kobe Bryant & The Mamba Mentality: Symphony of Greatness

Dear reader,

"Success Leaves Clues" proudly presents the new edition of the series and the second book about Kobe Bryant and The Mamba Mentality.

The first one, *"Kobe Bryant: Success Mindset,"* serves as a light-read action guide. In it, the focus is on the self-development of the reader. Through a series of guiding questions, exercises, and personal examples from Kobe Bryant's life, readers could come up with a personal action plan for success. The book is designed as a learning experience for the readers. In many ways, *"Kobe Bryant: Success Mindset"* is all about the reader.

''Kobe Bryant & The Mamba Mentality: Symphony of Greatness'' is different. This book is about Kobe Bryant, yet, it is for the reader.

This book is all about Kobe's ascension into eternity. It reveals and breaks down the elements of The Mamba Mentality that play together in perfect symphony, crafting the legend of the Great Kobe Bryant. In many ways, "Kobe Bryant & The Mamba Mentality is a case study of Greatness.

Before we embark on the exploration of the unique mentality which made Kobe Bryant the extraordinary winner in the game of life, we have to answer a question:

What is the Mamba Mentality?

Throughout the years, many have associated it with hard work and discipline. As you will discover later in this book, The Mamba Mentality goes much deeper than this surface-level observation. The Mamba Mentality is the multi-layered mindset of Greatness. Indeed, just like Kobe Bryant, The Mamba Mentality evolved over all these years.

Simply put, **The Mamba Mentality is the way of life, a journey into Greatness.**

On our journey of light, we can learn from the man himself and do what Kobe Bryant inspired us to do: Follow our curious spirit and learn by asking the right questions.

What were Kobe's personal values and beliefs, and how they've led to his Greatness?

After more than five years of studying Kobe Bryant and more than six intensive months in production development, **Kobe**

***Bryant & The Mamba Mentality: Symphony of Greatness* intends to answer the above question.**

For those looking for success clues, there is an abundance of those sprinkled throughout the entire book. After all, each chapter is based on a particular clue of Greatness. Each of those clues offers a glimpse into the mind and character of the one and only Kobe Bryant.

In addition, the clues reflect Kobe's life philosophy, revealing the connection between Kobe Bryant and his renowned mentality of winning and success.

The only way to present Kobe Bryant and his journey to Greatness is through stories. After all, Kobe was a storyteller, believing stories could transform society and move humanity forward into a brighter future.

In '*Kobe Bryant & The Mamba Mentality: Symphony of Greatness,*' you'll experience stories from various perspectives and points of view at different times throughout his life. On this journey, we'll revisit some of Kobe's most glorious moments in time and analyze them through the prism of his values and beliefs.

In addition, we'll take a look behind the curtain and investigate the connection between the events and life circumstances that shaped his iconic mindset, known as *The Mamba Mentality.*

Kobe Bryant & The Mamba Mentality: The Symphony of Greatness Roadmap

I. Origin Story
Looking back at Kobe's life, from the moment he was born into this world, Kobe Bryant seemed like he was predestined for Greatness. Even the most hardcore fans know that Kobe grew up in Italy, which he considered home.

We'll travel back in time and explore Kobe's upbringing and relationship with his family, especially his father, Joe Bryant. Joe was the man responsible for helping Kobe discover and channel his love for the game of basketball.

In this chapter, we get to witness the rise of the legend.

II. The Power of Solitude & Introspection
Since the moment he emerged in the NBA as the prodigy, Kobe has been a loner. Once he got to the NBA, solitude, and introspection were Kobe's superpowers.

In this chapter, we'll explore Bryant's decision to retire from the game and his discovery of a new calling in life. Through the practice of self-awareness, his spiritual rituals, and long introspection sessions, Kobe Bryant discovered a gift lying deep within him.

Here, we'll answer the question: *What were Kobe's personal development rituals, and how he used solitude to propel himself to the land of the immortals?*

III. Personal Mastery

Before he became the Master, Kobe had to learn how to be a student of the game first. Throughout his entire glorious career, Bryant was blessed and fortunate to have incredible teachers and mentors. Early on his journey, Kobe met a man who taught him the value of '*The Beginners Mind.*'

In this chapter, we'll break down Kobe's workout and practice regimen that made him one of the Greatest. On his journey to mastery, Kobe Bryant did things differently than anyone else.

Here, we'll revisit the event that served as the genesis of **The Mamba Mentality.** The humiliation 12-year-old Kobe experienced shook him to the core. He experienced a genuine paradigm shift.... And things were never the same again.

IV. The Identity & The Role of Alter-Ego

In this chapter, we'll relive the darkest moments of Kobe's life, including the battle for his family, freedom, and justice.

In 2003, a single incident sent Kobe Bryant down the path of self-discovery and self-recreation. However, the dreadful circumstances of his personal life catalyzed the emergence of his Alter Ego. Here, we'll break down the character of The Black Mamba and how it changed the landscape of the game.

V. Uncompromising Integrity

Kobe Bryant was a man with a specific code of conduct. **Kobe Bryant was a man who always stood up for what he believed in.** Driven by his personal beliefs and convictions, Kobe Bryant lived in accordance with his personal integrity.

Over the years, naturally, Kobe Bryant evolved. Yet, his fundamental beliefs remained unchanged and were even fortified by his maturation, experience, and, ultimately, wisdom.

In addition, we'll explore how the clash of opposing ideologies led to the rise & fall of the most dynamic duo in sports history.

VI. Relentless Desire & Mental Warfare
Kobe Bryant & The Mamba Mentality is synonymous with ferocious intensity, a drive to compete, and the unwavering desire to win.

In this chapter, we'll examine the thread between Bryant's desire to win and his ability to do anything necessary to achieve victory. Kobe's understanding of human psychology, combined with his intelligence and ruthless approach to basketball, made him a genuinely feared and dreaded opponent for any player on any given night.

Terrifying on both ends of the court, he had the same intensity in his game, combined with an equal desire to win, as *arguably the greatest player ever — Michael Jordan.* MJ is the epitome of the ultimate winner and champion. In fact, to any basketball player coming into the NBA league, Jordan was the benchmark for Greatness.

VII. Evolution & Leadership
In 2008, Bryant underperformed on the grandest stage and under the brightest lights.

Yet, Kobe's greatest defeat taught him a priceless lesson about compassion, empathy, and leadership. After the heartbreaking loss against his arch-rival, Kobe's inner ideal of Greatness changed.

He realized being the greatest player meant being the best leader to those around him. Suddenly, the game of basketball was so much more to Kobe.

Embracing the new challenge, Kobe Bryant was on a quest to inspire Greatness in his teammates.

VIII. Eternal Legacy: Greatness Echoes into Eternity

In the last stages of his career, Kobe understood the nature of the game is to evolve. He believed the nature of basketball reflects the nature of life itself. After his retirement from basketball, Kobe Bryant did his best to pass on knowledge, wisdom, and inspiration to the next generation.

In the last chapter, we are on the mission of revealing the answer to the final question: What does it take to be truly Great?

1

Origin Story

> *"Heroes come and go, but legends are forever."*

The first step on our journey of exploration takes us back around fifty years in the past.

In 1975, the Vietnam War ended. In 1975, one of the first blockbuster films, Jaws, was released. In 1975, the world saw Jimmy Hoffa for the last time.

In 1975, a man found himself at the crossroads of life.

After two years of playing collegiate basketball, **Joe Bryant got the opportunity of a lifetime**. He could turn professional and go directly to the NBA, the land of the basketball greats. On the other hand, two more years of development could ensure him a much better chance of succeeding once he got into the league.

Joe Bryant made a decision that would forever change his career trajectory and affect the rest of his life.

He decided to turn professional, and he declared for the draft lottery. Back in the 70s, there weren't a lot of college 'dropouts' in the NBA. The conventional wisdom was for a player to finish college before stepping on the wooden court with the big boys. (In fact, more than 20 years later, another Bryant shattered the false and fragile narrative when he joined the NBA as a 17-year-old.)

Philadelphia native Joe could've stayed at his local *La Salle* University for two more years to further develop as a player and improve his game. Staying at the college level meant regular playing time, which is a critical factor in the development of any young player, particularly those transitioning from collegiate to NBA basketball.

Despite the risks, Joe, who averaged 22 points and 12 rebounds as a sophomore, decided to go all in and cash in on his talent immediately.

In many regards, Joe Bryant was a player ahead of his time. Nicknamed 'JellyBeans,' Joe Bryant led the local *La Salle* University to decent success in college basketball. From the moment he stepped on the court, it was clear that *Joe Bryant had the game.*

As a junior, he dominated the competition. Fast, strong, agile, and quite technical, the 6ft9 power forward, Bryant drew nationwide attention by his sophomore year. He loved playing with a ball in his hand. Joe was skillful, had incredible court vision, and had a solid jump shooter. In addition, he was tall, lean, and athletic.

Yet, Joe's gifts were his curse. Joe Bryant was too big to play guard and too small to be a center under the basket.

Back in the 70s, basketball was almost a different sport. The game had a much slower tempo, and big men had to be close to the basket. Back in those days, centers wouldn't move much. On the contrary, they would position themselves under the basket, waiting for an assist for a simple lay-up. Big men had to be physical and aggressive. They had to leave dribbling and shooting for the 'smaller' men at the shooter's position.

Back then, it was inconceivable for centers to shoot and handle the ball. (The league's landscape would almost radically shift with the emergence of Magic Johnson in the late 70s and early 80s. Retrospectively, all Joe had to do was be patient and focus on playing regular basketball, even at the collegiate level.)

Once he arrived, Joe was often on the bench with limited playing time. In his first two seasons with the Philadelphia 76ers, Joe averaged 16 and 10 minutes per game, respectively. Various reasons and circumstances played a significant role in Bryant's basketball development. From the moment he arrived, his basketball growth was stunted. In turn, his confidence began to dwindle.

Unfortunately for Joe Bryant, he failed to adapt to the game at the highest level.

Joe spent eight years in the league and never reached the heights many predicted him years ago. He was a decent player and a solid bench contributor throughout his NBA career, which saw him put on jerseys of the *Philadelphia 76ers, San Diego Clippers, and Houston Rockets*. Despite being a reliable scorer whenever he played, his coaches didn't have faith in him. Joe never really got the chance to showcase his full talent throughout his entire NBA career.

At the end of the 1982 season, 28-year-old Joe Bryant was at the crossroads of his life. Once again, he had to make a choice.

It was crystal clear that Joe had no place in the NBA other than to be a bench warmer, at best. Joe could drop down into the minor league, where he could play comfortably for many years before retiring. On the other hand, the prospect of competing against the best players outside the United States offered all the allure Joe needed to sway his decision.

After all, despite his underwhelming NBA career, Joe Bryant was a fierce competitor in need of a challenge. Deep down, he knew he had more to offer to the game of basketball. With the unwavering support from his wife, Pamela, **Joe decided to go all in once again.**

While still in his physical prime, Joe chose to take his talent to Europe. Together with his family, he started a new chapter of life more than five thousand miles away from home.

In Italy, he played for *AMG Sebastiani Rieti, Standa Reggio Calabria, Olimpia Pistoia*, and *Reggiana*. He played with much success for another nine years before ending his career at 37. Wherever he went during his time abroad, Joe Bryant was the best player on the team.

Joe played the game just like he wanted: with the ball in his hands and the freedom to direct offense. Throughout his entire career abroad, he was remembered as a fearless scorer and ruthless competitor.

In Italy, life was a revelation for Joe. He enjoyed every second of it. Life turned out to be better than he could ever imagine. Unlike in the US, in Italy, he would play once a week, and most of his time, he spent with his family.

Joe soon noticed that his son, much like a father, fell in love with basketball. Their bond only grew stronger over time, and *Joe immediately recognized the seed of future greatness in his son.*

Because of the lighter schedule compared to the one in the US, Joe was a present father figure in Kobe's life. (However, as a parent, Joe made sure never to force or pressure his children, teaching them the value of independence.)

Joe was Kobe's first role model, coach, and mentor. Growing up, Kobe idolized his father, wanting to be like him. Joe Bryant played a pivotal role during Kobe's crucial development period, teaching him the fundamentals of the game.

As a player, Joe Bryant played his game, and he realized his potential. As a man, he gave his children the greatest gift any parent could give to a child: The gift of life filled with opportunity and abundance.

Ultimately, Joe's decision to move to Italy proved to be the right

one. With it, Joe Bryant set in motion a chain of events that led to the emergence of one of the greatest players ever.

> "My mom was there on a daily basis. She was the anchor of the home. My dad was always there as a father figure. He was there in those critical moments of my development.
>
> They instilled in me the importance of imagination and curiosity. They told me: **'You can accomplish anything you want, but if you want to accomplish anything in life, you will have to put in the work.'**
>
> They taught me the value of hard work and imagination from an early age. When you are a kid thinking the world is your oyster, and everything is possible if you put in the work, you grow up with that fundamental belief."
>
> – Kobe Bryant on his family and earliest childhood.

The Rise of the Prodigy

Born on August 23, 1978, in Philadelphia, Kobe Bryant was the third and the youngest child in the family. Although too young to remember, by the age of four, he lived in three different cities within the US.

However, Kobe's earliest memories are of his first home in Italy.

His mother, **Pamela Bryant**, was the anchor of the family. She understood the life and sacrifices needed in professional sports, as her younger brother John played in the NBA. She wholeheartedly supported Joe in achieving his goals, while her mission was to keep their foundation, their home, in order.

Pamela was a devoted Catholic. She and Joe made sure to raise children in the same faith. For the Bryant's, family always comes first. As the siblings were just three years apart, Kobe was especially close to his two older sisters, Sharia and Shaya.

One of the things they did traditionally as a family was watching basketball games on TV.

Dressed in the appropriate sports jersey, Kobe couldn't just watch the game. He wanted to participate. He was only three, and he could barely walk, but he would not be deterred. Kobe would stand in the living room, shooting the ball at his little basket.

Like any other child, Kobe had a vivid imagination.

He instinctively emulated the players on the screen. If they shot the ball, he would pretend to shoot the ball. If they passed the ball, he would follow the very next second. When they took a time out, he reluctantly sat down on the floor, carefully listening to what the coach had to say. Young Kobe shared the same love for the game of basketball as his old man.

Naturally, Kobe's earliest role model and basketball idol was his father. Recognizing his son's desire to be around him and to be around the game, Joe gave his best to introduce Kobe to basketball. Once they've settled in Italy, he would take Kobe to each of his practices and take him to official team matches.

Kobe would sit on the bench nearby, mesmerized by the game of basketball. He sat on the bench watching in awe as his father battled on the court, fighting fierce competition during the golden age of Italian basketball.

Little Kobe couldn't stay still, and he would start helping out by mopping the floor between the game intervals. Showing his entrepreneurial spirit from a young age, Kobe Bryant cut his first sponsorship deal with the owner of Joe's second club in Italy, Olimpia Pistoia, to wear a sweatshirt branded with their business when he cleaned the court. In return, the owner agreed to Kobe's request and bought him a new red bicycle.

Once he wiped down the court, he often picked up a basketball and dazzled the crowd with his "Kobe Show," only leaving the court when the game officials kicked him off. The crowd would stay put and stare at the boy shooting at the basket. Some cheered him on, some chuckled and laughed, and others yelled at him to move from the court. In any case, the outside noise never bothered Kobe. Even as a boy, he was unfazed by the crowd. Kobe was locked in and focused on the court and what was happening right in front of him.

During his earliest formative years, Kobe spent most of his time around the game of basketball. When he was six, he received a present from his parents. Kobe got his first leather ball, and from that moment on, he would dribble it anywhere he went.

Coincidentally, from the moment he got his first basketball, Kobe Bryant discovered the allure of solitude. He realized he could play his favorite game all by himself. Kobe quickly developed a routine where he'd come from school, do all the homework for the day, and ensure he prepared everything needed for tomorrow. As soon as he was finished, Kobe would hop on his little red bicycle and ride to the nearby park to play basketball.

Aside from basketball, Kobe Bryant developed a passion for sports movies, documentaries, and biographies of famous athletes. Kobe loved watching NBA films and docu-series often produced by NBA Entertainment, the production arm of the NBA. **From the earliest age, Kobe was drawn to greatness, devouring any sports literature, looking for clues to their success.**

More by chance than a choice, little Kobe took a keen interest in other sports, mainly soccer.

In Italy, soccer is a national sport and a sport where they've traditionally had the most success. For many Italians, soccer is a religion on its own. Kobe soon realized that soccer is the only sport kids play in parks and local playgrounds. Kobe would go to a local playground with the basketball under his arm every day, hoping that someone would play with him. Once he got there, he quickly realized he had only two choices: Play soccer with other kids or pack up and go home.

For Kobe, especially during his early childhood, the game of soccer was an essential vehicle for making his first friends in a foreign land.

Growing up in Italy had a tremendous impact on Kobe's development as a person and as a basketball player.

From day one, Kobe was immersed in the Italian culture as he entered the first grade with other Italian kids. As Kobe described it years later, it was a *'sink or swim'* moment, which his imagination made into a competitive challenge. Being a naturally curious child, Kobe was eager to learn and quickly picked up a new language. Within a few months, he was speaking fluent Italian.

As Kobe Bryant recalls his earliest memories in Italy, he noted that as a black family living in Europe, the Bryants were considered both curiosities and celebrities.

> *"People treat others as equals there. They don't mistrust each other. They say hello when they see you on the street. And family — family is big there."*
>
> *- Kobe Bryant, in a 1996 interview with the Philadelphia Inquirer.*

When Kobe was old enough, Joe Bryant allowed his son to play organized basketball. At age 8, Kobe joined his first basketball team as he became a new member of the Reggio Calabria youth ranks.

From the basketball standpoint, Italy is renowned for the system that creates and promotes talented youngsters. That system allows young players to develop at their own pace without unnecessary pressure. Under the watchful eye of coaches and trainers, youngsters learn about the game's tactical side and have the time to improve any weakness in their game.

On the other side of the ocean, the goal is to win at all costs, starting from the junior level. In the US, coaches are under pressure to deliver results, even to the detriment of talent development. Because of that, young players in the US usually don't have the same luxury of steady development as their European peers.

(Decades later and way after he became a superstar, Kobe Bryant was adamant about the flawed youth basketball system in the US, and he pointed to Europe's counterpart as the possible solution.)

Fortunately for Kobe, growing up, he had access to some of the best coaches. Being the son of great Joe Bryant, a bonafide superstar in Europe, meant that little Kobe had access to many great former and current players. Naturally, he seized every opportunity he could to learn about the game.

Driven by his insatiable curiosity and a desire to learn the game of basketball, Bryant's favorite hobby as a kid was studying the game through the old VHS tapes. Kobe's grandfather was a passionate fan of the NBA. He regularly mailed tapes with all the NBA games from his lofty collection. Even as a young boy, Kobe would watch the game as a professional, rewinding and focusing on a particular move he liked. He would then take his basketball and go to the park, where he'd practice those moves repeatedly until he could perform them unconsciously.

In pursuit of his basketball excellence, between the ages of 11 and 15, he would spend his summers in the US, playing basketball in a prominent *Sunny Hill Junior League* in Philadelphia.

By the time he was 11, Kobe was the best player in Italy for his age group. As he shared years later, he was better than the other kids in Italy because he was bigger and taller than everybody else and would play to his strengths.

Kobe relied on his natural physicality and size to win games, but the problem arose once he played against stronger and more physical opponents in the USA. Suddenly stripped of the most lethal weapon in his arsenal, he learned the invaluable life lesson the hard way.

> *"Son, whether you score 0, or you score 60, your mother and I are going to love you no matter what."*
> — *Joe Bryant comforting his crying son after Kobe's first basketball camp in the US.*

After the embarrassing experience, which served as a wake-up call for Kobe, he made a decision that would forever change his life: Never ever would he rely on his natural talent and physical ability to win games. **Instead, Kobe Bryant wowed to master the game from the foundation, starting with footwork.**

Grateful for the love and support from his parents despite the outcome, Kobe Bryant made a deal with himself to become the greatest basketball player of all time. Still just a teenager, Kobe promised himself that he would do anything and everything he could to achieve this goal.

With an oath came a newfound sense of purpose, followed by hard work and unparalleled commitment to the game of basketball.

By the time Kobe was 14, he already had a polished game with very few glaring weaknesses. He was the best player in his age group and well above that age limit. He often played with older kids, but the outcome was always the same: Total annihilation.

Just as Kobe thought life couldn't get any better, he received news that would soon set him up on a new path.

After 16 years of playing basketball, Joe Bryant decided to retire. Although they could've stayed in Italy, where they built a comfortable life, Joe and Pamela Bryant chose to move back to the US. One of the greatest fears both parents had was for their children to forget the English language, and that fear was the primary motivator for their return to America.

In 1991, the family moved back to Philadelphia, and Kobe enrolled in eighth grade at Bala Cynwyd Middle School.

The Decision That Forever Changed the Landscape of the NBA

The readjustment to life in the US was rough. Bryant had difficulty catching up with his peers in school. It took him a while to pick up on the slang and understand his new classmates.

Kobe felt like an outsider, which he certainly was. He dressed, talked, and thought differently than most of his peers. Ironically, Kobe felt like a foreigner again, this time in his own country. In Italy, he was an American in a foreign country. In the US, he was that 'Italian kid.'

He preferred his own company over anyone else's. He was a loner, and he enjoyed the solitude, yet those who remember him from those days claim he was friendly and always approachable. He didn't shy away from people. He just never bothered to try to fit in at any cost.

Kobe had other priorities.

> *"Just 5 minutes after seeing him in action, I turned to my assistant and said: 'This kid is a pro. He worked harder than anyone else, and he set an example for the rest of the team. It was easy to coach him because he was eager to learn and improve his game."*
>
> *— Greg Downer, Lower Marion High School Basketball Coach.*

The only thing on Kobe's mind was basketball.
He wanted to prove himself against his peers, especially those considered the best in the country. Instead of partying like his classmates, Kobe spent his time practicing. He would stay late in the gym and work on the particular aspect of the play he would use in the upcoming game. Kobe would repeat the move thousands of times until he'd perfected it.

His reputation spread like wildfire.

For Kobe Bryant, there was only one thing that mattered. He was obsessed with becoming the best basketball player ever. His work ethic, dedication to the craft, and his insane performances quickly garnered Bryant national attention.

Kobe's high school career was nothing short of spectacular. He was a member of Lower Merion High School in Ardmore, located in the Philadelphia suburb of Lower Merion. Even as a freshman, Kobe joined a varsity team and quickly showed glimpses of future greatness. After a rocky first year, where the team compiled a losing 4–20 record, the Aces achieved a 77–13 record the following three years, with Bryant playing all five positions. He averaged 31.1 points, 10.4 rebounds, 5.2 assists, 3.8 blocks, and 2.3 steals during his junior year.

Kobe was named Pennsylvania Player of the Year while also earning a fourth-team *Parade* All-American nomination, attracting attention from college recruiters in the process. Duke, Michigan, North Carolina, and Villanova were at the top of his list.

By 1996, the youngster was a basketball sensation, and his name was all over the media headlines. Kobe was dubbed 'the prodigy' by the media, a narrative that was only fortified by the prestigious awards he won, such as *Gatorade National Player of the Year, Naismith Prep Player of the Year, McDonald's All-American, and First-team Parade All-American.*

In addition, the media started drawing comparisons with the all-time greats such as **Michael Jordan** and **Magic Johnson**, adding to Kobe's mystique. However, many believed this young man to be nothing more than hype, as the rumors began spreading about Kobe skipping college and making a jump directly to the NBA.

In his senior year of high school, Bryant led the Aces to their first state championship in 53 years.

During the run, he averaged 30.8 points, 12 rebounds, 6.5 assists, 4 steals, and 3.8 blocked shots, leading the Aces to a 31–3 record. Despite his young age, many NBA teams expressed their interest in Kobe, especially after word of his impressive NBA workouts began spreading around the league.

NBA workouts are usually a series of training sessions and practices a player goes through individually and with a potential team. It is an opportunity for a player to showcase his talents in front of the team's executives, and for many, it's an opportunity to seize the moment and make their dreams come true.

In 1996, Kobe had multiple workouts with various teams in the league, but after one particular workout, Kobe knew where he belonged. Due to his father's connections in Philadelphia, Kobe had a workout with the Philadelphia 76ers, where he had an opportunity to play 1–1 against arguably the best college player at the time and a *future NBA superstar — Jerry Stackhouse.*

Jerry was recently declared a National Player of the Year by *Sports Illustrated* and earned first-team All-America and All-ACC honors, and he was touted as the next *Michael Jordan*. Coming to the league as the best college player in the US, Jerry Stackhouse was the #3 draft pick in the 1995 NBA draft. Jerry was expected to lead the 76ers franchise for years to come, and Kobe bested him.

Although Stackhouse outright refused to admit it publicly throughout the rest of his career, according to various unofficial sources, Kobe dominated in a 1–1 game, beating the future All-Star pretty comfortably, leaving Philadelphia's coaching staff and executives in awe.

As the 1996 draft was approaching, Bryant was one of the most-watched high school players in the country. Scouts, sports reporters, and high school basketball fans all flocked to the school to watch him play. ***ESPN*** and other big media outlets covered Kobe's every move, adding to the pressure until the day of the inevitable decision.

A few months before the draft, 17-year-old Kobe Bryant held a press conference in his Lower Merion high school gym, where he announced his intentions to the world.

Seemingly unfazed by the gravity of the moment, with all the swag and confidence in the world, and with sunglasses on his forehead, Kobe stepped up and declared:

"My name is Kobe Bryant, and I've decided to take my talents to...

... I've decided to skip college and take my talents straight to the NBA."

Kobe's decision caused an uproar throughout the league, with many past and present players expressing doubts and reservations about his chances in the best league in the world. Once he made his decision, Kobe was bombarded with a hailstorm of controversy.

The media at the time heavily criticized Kobe's demeanor at that press conference, calling a teenager arrogant and naive for daring to step up with the big boys. They expressed skepticism while pointing out that only seven players in history came to the league straight from high school. All of those players were strong, big men who were generally favored in the league.

On the other hand, Kobe was a guard, perceived by the public at the time as a scrawny kid unable to compete physically with much older men. Despite some negative reactions, the league was undoubtedly brewing with excitement about the upcoming prospect from Lower Marion.

Regardless of the reaction, Kobe Bryant couldn't care less about the public perception and opinions. He was on a mission to become the best player who ever played the game, and in Kobe's mind, he was undeniable.

Ever since he fell in love with basketball as a toddler, he dreamed of playing in the NBA. Years later, when asked to explain his decision, Kobe said:

"One day, when it's all said and done, and my career is over, I want to be able to look back without regret. My goal was always to play and compete against the best.

People go to college so that they can have a job. I already had a job. I play basketball."

Many people back then believed his decision seemed hasty and outright wrong. However, before making such a crucial step, Kobe taught long and hard about his future. Bryant was a gifted student, and he certainly had the grades for any college in the state, but his heart yearned for a challenge.

On a historic night in June 1996, Kobe Bryant entered the league as the 13th pick in the draft lottery. Originally selected by the **Charlotte Hornets**, they traded him just hours later for **Vlade Divac**, the starting center of the **Los Angeles Lakers.** This trade made a lot of noise and commotion, yet Kobe remained calm. Jerry West, the man behind the logo of the NBA and a general manager of the LA franchise at the time, saw the almost unlimited potential of this young man.

On that fateful night in June 1996, little did the world know that it was witnessing the birth of an icon. With his signature smile, Kobe Bryant stepped into the spotlight, where he would stay until the end of his NBA career in 2016.

2

The Power of Solitude & Introspection

> *"Mamba Mentality comes from the foundation of being self-aware of things that are happening within your life that you can use as fuel to propel you forward. That's the foundation, and from then on, it's the constant search for answers because that's how you get better at whatever it is that you are doing. Mamba Mentality is the way of life."*

In 2002, Fox Sports aired a documentary on Kobe Bryant. The movie, part of the series entitled *"Beyond Glory,"* focuses on Kobe's life journey, emergence in the league, and the historic Laker's success. They just won their third championship in a row, cementing their position as one of the greatest NBA teams ever.

The documentary features many people from Kobe's life, including his coach, ***Phil Jackson.***

Phil is the man who revolutionized the modern game of basketball. 11x NBA champion is known as the ***"Zen Master"*** and is renowned for a holistic approach to coaching influenced by Eastern philosophy. He rejected the moniker, believing his approach to life and basketball is about mindfulness.

Indeed, Phil is a man who showed Kobe how to work on his mind. He showed Bryant how to apply these Eastern philosophies as a practical tool for improvement. It is no wonder why he credits Phil Jackson as an important mentor figure and a great teacher of the game. Indeed, if someone could give us precise insight into the mind of Kobe Bryant, it would be Phil Jackson.

Midway through the sports documentary, Phil Jackson told us: **"Kobe is a man who loves solitude, and he enjoys being in his own world. ''**

* * *

Crossroads Moment: The Road to Retirement and The Journey into the Unknown

In November 2015, Kobe Bryant put the NBA on notice as he announced his plan to retire at the end of the season. After 20 years in the league, he felt it was time to walk away from the game. It was, truly, the end of an era. Records shattered and respect well-earned, Kobe said goodbye to his first love.

His body suffered a myriad of injuries, particularly over the last few seasons. In fact, 37-year-old Kobe hadn't finished a season healthy since 2012. During the final three years of his career, Kobe Bryant spent more time in rehab and physio room than he did with his team.

We, the fans, knew the moment would come, eventually. No man has ever beaten Father Time. As an athlete at the highest level of sports, the best you can hope for is to prolong the inevitable. Kobe certainly did manage to do it, but he paid the price once he did.

He worked as hard as ever to return to the court, just to be welcomed by another misfortune. As various injuries piled up, his body began sending signals. It just couldn't keep up with his mind.

Despite all the setbacks in the final few years of his career and his advanced age, Kobe Bryant was still the best player on the LA team. During his last year as a Laker, Kobe had multiple triple-double games. He had a few memorable moments, including his performance in his final game against the *Utah Jazz*, where he scored 60 points in *Staples Centar*.

Undoubtedly, Kobe could still play at a high level, but not at the standard of excellence he set for himself. Once that thought breached into his conscious mind, he knew the time had come. Kobe decided it was time to say goodbye to his first love. He left the game in good hands, and he retired as a legend. Now, it was time to start a new chapter in life.

THE POWER OF SOLITUDE & INTROSPECTION

During the last few years of his career, Bryant discovered a new calling.

As a man who thrived in solitude throughout his entire life, Kobe always enjoyed the allure of isolation. After all, it was only in those moments when he was alone that he could find the answers he was seeking. For a short while, he wondered about the next chapter of his life, the one after his basketball career.

While recovering from various injuries, starting with a torn Achilles heel in 2013, Kobe was forced to face the uncertainty about his future. He realized his playing career could be over at any given moment, and more than anything, Kobe Bryant wanted to finish his career and retire under his terms.

The last thing Bryant wanted was to linger in the NBA more than he should, being a shell of his former self. By doing that, Kobe knew he would taint the image of greatness he carefully curated over the years and decades.

Less than a month after his retirement and the iconic performance in his last-ever basketball, Kobe was a guest at the prestigious *independent economic think tank **Milken Institute.***

In a fascinating conversation with ***Jim Gray***, a famous longtime sportscaster for *'Showtime,' 'Fox,'* and other prominent media outlets, Kobe shared a personal story of self-discovery:

> *"I was fortunate in the unfortunate, having all these injuries. With the Achilles, my shoulder and knees...*

I was fortunate because it gave me a lot of time to think. It gave me a lot of time to sit and reflect, and it gave me a lot of time to realize that: 'Man, my career could be over right now, and with all of that work that you've done trying to figure out what comes next...You are unprepared for.'

I kept thinking over and over again, asking the wrong question:
What is the biggest industry I can get into that has the biggest upside?

Wrong question.

Then, I started asking myself a different question:
What do you love to do the most?"

Through the practice of self-awareness, his spiritual rituals, and long introspection sessions, Kobe Bryant discovered a gift lying deep within him. All he had to do was to unwrap that gift, and as he did, he discovered his purpose.

"My passion is storytelling. I love telling stories. I can't go away from that. This is what I am excited to do. I am fortunate to have another passion outside of the game of basketball."

The process of realization didn't come overnight for Kobe. On the contrary, he admits it took him more than 15 years. Always curious about life, around the age of 20, he started contemplating the next step in life.

He knew that the basketball career, no matter how great it turned out to be, had an expiry date attached to it. Back then, he had no idea what would come next. Fortunately and relatively early on in life, Kobe Bryant recognized the things he naturally gravitated toward. Aside from the game of basketball, Kobe certainly had other interests, hobbies, and aspirations.

Despite his dedication to basketball and rigorous schedule, Kobe had more than enough time to try out different things while still playing. He was naturally curious about life and was not afraid to dive head-first into a completely new endeavor. Since joining the Lakers as a teenager, Kobe has been eager to experiment and explore.

He tried his hands at music and acting before realizing he wasn't interested in the show business side of the lifestyle.

Bryant has had various successful business ventures, especially after his playing career. Kobe certainly had a mind for business. He was making connections as easily as he once scored points.

Notably, Bryant established **Kobe Inc.** with the idea of owning and growing brands in the sports industry. The initial investment was a 10% stake in the *Bodyarmor SuperDrink* company for $6 million in March 2014. With *The Coca-Cola Company* purchasing a minority stake in the company in August 2018, the valuation of **Bryant's stake rose to approximately $200 million.**

As successful as those various side projects were, Kobe didn't feel like a businessman, entrepreneur, or venture capitalist. Aside from the occasional thrill of winning in business, his heart wasn't fully in it. All he longed to do was to tell stories. By the time his playing career ended, he was ready and at peace. Kobe had a clear vision of the future.

His mission was to inspire the next generation of athletes, and he did so through storytelling, his new vehicle of expression.

At first, not everyone around him saw the path he chose to walk on as a viable next step in life. Bryant remembers a lot of 'funny looks' and 'raised eyebrows' once he announced his decision to the world. Interestingly, Kobe received a similar reaction all those years ago when he proclaimed his intention to be the greatest basketball player that ever lived.

He had all the support from his loved ones, which was all he needed. With the same intensity, dedication, and meticulous approach, Kobe poured his heart and soul into the craft of storytelling.

Ever the student, Bryant reached out to the best of the best, to those the world considers masters.

Famously, he cold-called **George R. R. Martin**, the author of the series of epic fantasy novels *A Song of Ice and Fire*, which was adapted into the Emmy Award-winning HBO series *Game of Thrones.* They spent a few hours conversing about fantasy world-building and creating relatable characters in a story.

Bryant also reached out to **J. K. Rowling, the author of Harry Potter**, a seven-volume children's fantasy series published from

1997 to 2007. The series has sold over 500 million copies, been translated into at least 70 languages, and spawned a global media franchise, including films and video games.

At the same time, Kobe approached his new endeavors with the utmost commitment, learning the business side of his new passion. Just like cold-called masters of literature, he did the same with *Oprah Winfrey, Arianna Huffington*, *Jony Ive* of Apple, and Nike's *Mark Parker.*

Bryant relied on his personal network and the connections he built through the years. His goal was to assemble the best people in their respective roles and to unite the team behind the same vision for the future. Just like he led the mighty Los Angeles Lakers not so long ago, once again, Kobe found himself in a leadership role.

Soon after, Kobe founded a production company and got to work.

Bryant launched *'Granity Studios;' a* multimedia original content company focused on creating new ways to tell stories around sports. *Kobe partnered with award-winning writers, producers, and illustrators to awaken the imagination of young athletes and foster emotional and mental development that allows them to reach their full potential.*

When Kobe Bryant announced his retirement, he did so in style.

He wrote an open letter to the *Player's Tribune.* Instead of formally announcing his retirement, Kobe told us a story. Less than two years after leaving the game of basketball, Bryant was nominated for his first award, the most prestigious one in the filmmaking industry.

In typical mamba fashion, Kobe Bryant announced his arrival, not with a dunk but with a heartwarming short film. Based on his retirement letter, **Dear Basketball** tells a touching story of a boy who says goodbye to his first love.

On March 4th, 2018, Kobe's first film won an Academy Award for Best Animated Short Film at the 90th Academy Awards. Bryant became the first African-American to win the **Academy Award for Best Animated Short Film**. He was also the first former professional athlete to be nominated for and win an Academy Award. In addition, just a couple of months before, Bryant won the **Sports Emmy Award for Outstanding Post-Produced Graphic Design.**

Kobe Bryant showed us what the human spirit is capable of, inspiring us to dream and work passionately on what we love. Through his personal example, he showed us that life doesn't have to be a linear experience.

> *"I was personal about it when I wrote 'Dear Basketball,' but that is the true challenge of finding out what comes next. The challenge of finding something you love to do every bit as much as you loved your first passion. That is the challenge for us athletes.*
>
> *Unfortunately for us athletes, we've been pigeonholing,*

thinking we can only be one thing. When I retired, people said: 'He is too competitive; he is not going know what to do with himself. He is going to have to come back.'

I took that as a personal challenge. They thought I was this one-dimensional person; all I know is how to dribble a ball, shoot it, play basketball, and compete at that level.

I will never come back to the game, ever. I am here to show people that we can do much more than that. Creating this business, winning an Oscar, and other awards show other athletes that there is more to life."

* * *

The Trait of The Great: Solitude as a Tool For Personal Development

Throughout most of his life, Kobe was a loner.

Since his earliest childhood in Italy, he discovered the allure of solitude. When the family moved to Italy, Kobe spent most of his time alone. Understandably, he was different from the other kids, and he struggled through the initial adaptation period.

His father's career dictated his early childhood. As soon as Kobe settled in a new place and made new friends, Joe Bryant moved to another club in another city. The same cycle happened over and over again. During their time in Italy, the family lived in three different cities throughout the country.

Instead of trying to make new friends and fit in, Kobe took the ball to the park. All by himself, Kobe was lost doing what he loves the most—playing basketball. From age six, he knew that no matter what happened around him, he could always turn to basketball for comfort.

The game of basketball he played in solitude was the only constant in Kobe's early life.

Most importantly, he enjoyed being alone. He didn't have to depend on others, as he could always take the ball and play by himself. When playing alone, he usually tried out new moves he picked from watching and studying NBA games.

Isolated from the rest of the world, solitude provided him the opportunity to become a better basketball player, and that was all the incentive Kobe Bryant needed.

As he got a little older, he used solitude as a tool for personal growth.

In these quiet moments, Kobe would check in with himself, often reflecting on the day behind him or simply contemplating life. During his teenage years, he developed another practice that would help immensely on his road to greatness: the practice of *writing and journaling.*

Research has found that writing is one of those life skills with

a significant ROI (return on investment), as a consistent act of writing makes one a better thinker. Great writing requires observation, reflection, analysis, and an artful presentation of information. Science has shown that the act of writing significantly improves critical thinking ability. Critical thinking is the capability to think clearly and rationally, understanding the logical connection between ideas.

Once he started thinking critically about the game, Kobe noticed a drastic improvement on the court.

Over time, he became more diligent in his preparation and thoughtful about the game. He was studying and dissecting the game with surgical efficiency. Kobe realized he could easily keep track of his progress in basketball, but also in life. Once he became aware of the benefits of writing and journaling, Bryant quickly made it into a habit, which became a joyful activity he looked forward to.

However, Kobe's love for solitude almost cost him a relationship with his new teammates in Los Angeles.

One of the most difficult challenges he faced was adjusting to the lifestyle of the NBA superstar. Coming into the league at 17, he wasn't legally allowed to drink, even if he wanted to. Yet Kobe had no desire to socialize outside of the basketball court.

Somehow, it was expected of Kobe to adjust his lifestyle and personal routines for the sake of the team. They expected him to join off-the-court activities such as visiting nightclubs and drinking champagne until the early morning hours. Unsurprisingly, he wasn't interested in getting drunk or anything else that would even slightly deter him from his mission.

There was no place in the world where he would rather be than on the basketball court. If not on the court playing basketball, Bryant preferred to study the game, analyze the details, contemplate the information, meditate in silence, or visualize the game in front of his mind eye.

Once he got to the NBA, solitude and introspection were Kobe's superpowers. Yet, Bryant's preference for solitude and his aloof personality were a point of contention between him and his Lakers teammates for a better part of a decade. They thought he was weird due to his obsessive approach to the profession, his dedication to the game, and his habits and routines. The only 'redeeming quality' Kobe had in their eyes was hard to neglect. He was really that good at the game of basketball.

Kobe Bryant was an enigma to all of his teammates in the *Purple and Gold.* For the most part, however, they had a hard time understanding Kobe.

They simply wondered: **How can this kid spend so much time alone?**

The idea of voluntary solitude, for many, is the idea of voluntary torture. On the other hand, some believe that isolation is an esoteric ideal hardly to be achieved due to the modern-day lifestyle. In today's society, where productivity is often the primary measure of success, solitude is often a luxury many think they can't afford.

THE POWER OF SOLITUDE & INTROSPECTION

In our fast-paced, interconnected world, solitude is not a luxury. Solitude is a necessity. **The Mamba Mentality teaches us that solitude is an invaluable resource for those striving for Greatness.**

In solitude, we can cultivate imagination.

One of the greatest gifts we receive at birth is the power of imagination. Imagination is a powerful force we access at any point during our life journey. Imagination is the bridge between creativity and innovation.

Innovation is how we create a better society and, ultimately, evolve as a species. Great people who moved humanity forward and left a dent in the universe had the ability to harness and use the force of imagination. They did so by first embracing solitude and the power of introspection.

One of the many memorable photos of Kobe was the moment captured through the lens of **Andrew D. Bernstein**. Andy, as he was known in the NBA circles, has been a longtime LA Lakers photographer, and he followed Kobe's career from the beginning to end.

The iconic photograph dubbed **'The Thinker'** shows Kobe in Madison Square Garden, sitting on a bench in a changing room hours before the game. Andy took that photo during Bryant's final season, and the photograph captures the essence of the Mamba Mentality.

Sitting all alone, with his swollen knees, broken index finger on his shooting hand, and his feet inside of an ice tub — Kobe appears to be focused, yet he seems so distant from the reality of the present moment. He looks seemingly lost in his thoughts, drifting far away from the confines of the locker room.

Knowing what Kobe and the Mamba Mentality were all about, at that moment, he was most likely meditating and in control over the wandering mind.

Kobe learned how to control the mind through ***Meditation and Visualization, and he was an avid Mindfulness practitioner.*** Once he realized the importance of these practices and how much they elevate his game, bringing him a step closer to his goal of being the best ever, he adopted them without hesitation.

Naturally, his solitude was the only environment where he could successfully engage in these personal development practices.

He used solitude as a means to an end. The end goal was always to be one of the greatest ever. For Bryant, solitude was a way to constant improvement. In solitude, he could do his homework and preparation, which he always considered a critical part of the game.

Once he examined the opposing team, he would thoroughly analyze the way they play, their strategy and tactics, and their offensive and defensive tendencies. Once he gathered the necessary information from his research and study, he would move on to the next step.

Kobe would then proceed to visualize all the possible ways he could take advantage of any weakness in the opponent's

armor.

He allowed his mind and vivid imagination to run their course as he sat and visualized. He would observe the mind in silence. He would envision different ways to win, evaluating each path in his mind.

After meditating and visualizing, Kobe proceeded to the final step. He gave his visions the physical form by putting them on paper.

The stories of Bryant's unique preparation rituals are too many to count, but one particular experience shared by **Matt Barnes** encapsulates the brilliance of Kobe's mind and his preparation process.

"It was my first year with the Lakers. We were flying to Spain for a pre-season. It was a long flight, and everybody was sleeping on the plane. I remember seeing Kobe sitting still at the front of the plane. It looked to me as if he was writing something. At first, I thought he was writing rap lyrics or something like that.

I went to him, and as I approached him, I was shocked to see all these papers just scattered around. I remember one particular piece of paper had like 30 different basketball courts on it. He was all in, drawing and sketching different plays and positions.

He told me: 'I know I have to draw at least three people. I got the guy guarding me, the guy that's coming to double,

> *and then the help side. So, I am looking to see where you, Lamar, Pau, Ron, and Fish, are going to be open at all times.'*
>
> *I remember standing there and thinking... 'Yeah, this man is something else"*
> - ***Matt Barnes***, Bryant's LA Lakers Teammate (2010–2012)

Kobe often used isolation as a vehicle for self-reflection.

In silence, he could focus on cognitive, emotional, and behavioral self-evaluation. In solitude, he dealt with all his fears and doubts. After all, it was the solitude where he pondered his future and where he got answers. Near the end of his career, when he was recovering from various injuries, Bryant spent a lot of time thinking about his next step in life.

Apparently, there was no big 'AHA' moment of revelation. For Kobe, it was just a quiet realization of what has always been there. His passion for storytelling was always within him.

Yet, to make such a critical judgment, he had to invest a lot of time, energy, and effort to regularly check in with himself.

Like so many greats who came before and shaped the world we live in, **Kobe Bryant looked forward to moments in solitude. In his pursuit of greatness, solitude, introspection, and daily spiritual rituals helped him far beyond the wooden court.**

At the later stages of his career and during the recovery phase, he doubled down on spiritual growth practices, including writing and journaling, meditation and visualization, and mindfulness.

In 2018, Kobe shared wisdom on how he used solitude and introspection to improve his performance.

Kobe's Spiritual Rituals for Peak Performance

> *"I meditate every day. I do it in the morning for about 10–15 minutes. It's essential for me to do it because it sets me up for the rest of the day. It's like having an anchor. If I don't do it, I feel like I am constantly chasing the day, as opposed to being in control and dictating the day.*
>
> *I don't mean that you are calling all the shots on what comes forward, but it's about the fact that I am set and ready for whatever may come my way. I am calm about everything that comes my way. I get that from starting the day with meditation.*
>
> *For me, it's all about listening to my inner self.*
>
> *You sit in silence, and you allow all these thoughts to come forward. You get the chance to observe the self. Observe things that lay beneath the surface. I know it's hard to find the time to sit in silence, but you never pay attention to them if you don't.*
>
> *The reality is we are paying attention to so many things*

going on around us. We are constantly in some kind of a rush. We are constantly taking pictures and selfies to post on Instagram and other social media platforms. We constantly observe things around us that we don't take the time to observe what's on going on inside of ourselves.

In 1999, we got a new head coach by the name of Phil Jackson. He was really big on Mindfulness and Meditation. In all honesty, Phil didn't give us much of a choice. We had to do it. We would sit in our film room, and he'd turn the lights out, and we would meditate as a group.

He taught us a lot about mindfulness. For me, it connected right away because he was teaching mindfulness through something that I love and was extremely passionate about, which was the game of basketball.

He taught us through the lens of 'THIS' is going to help you 'HERE.' Naturally, I was curious about his teachings because I wanted to learn. Soon after, I saw the poise that we were playing with. We would remain calm in a hostile environment with a full arena yelling and screaming at us.

In high-pressure situations, these things had no effect on us. Why? Because we were never too high or too low, we were always just in the middle, facing the moment, ready for whatever came our way.''

3

Personal Mastery

"Everything I did, whether I watched a tv show, a documentary, books I read, people I talked to...Everything was done to learn how to become a better basketball player. Everything. When you have that point of view, the world becomes your library to help you become better at your craft."

In 2006, the LA Lakers were at a crossroads.

The team was just a year removed from the dreadful season where they didn't make the playoff for the first time in over a decade. The winning mentality that defined the team was seemingly lost. After firing two coaches in just one season, LA management made drastic changes. After unceremoniously leaving the franchise in 2004, *Phil Jackson* returned to the organization, taking the position at the helm.

In 2006, Kobe Bryant played as a man possessed.

Just a year prior, Kobe Bryant missed the playoff for the first time in his career. Despite posting his usual individual numbers, in 2005, Kobe's reputation was on the line. The year signified a drop in Bryant's overall status in the NBA, as he did not make the NBA All-Defensive Team and was also demoted to the All-NBA Third Team.

Despite the return of Phil Jackson, Kobe knew the rest of the team was sub-par. Bryant believed that the only way for LA to avoid the embarrassment of missing the playoff was for him to step to another level, which is precisely what he did.

The 2005/2006 NBA season marked one of the greatest scoring seasons in history.

That year, Kobe broke record after record. On December 20th, 2005, he accomplished something no one has in the modern game of basketball. *Against the Dallas Mavericks, Kobe scored 62 points in just three quarters.* Coming into the game's final quarter, Kobe Bryant singlehandedly outscored the entire Mavs team.

Bryan Shaw, Kobe's teammate from 1999–2003 and later the assistant manager for the Lakers from 2005–2011, remembers the historic game in Dallas. On that night, Shaw was on the sideline. Phil Jackson tasked Shaw with asking Bryant if he wanted to play in the fourth quarter. Bryant said no because it was a blowout, shocking Shaw.

"I told him: 'Look, man, not too many people can say

*they scored 70 points against another team. You've got
a chance to score 70. Man, you've got to play.'*

He looked at the scoreboard again, and he told me:

*'Nah, we're up 30. We don't need it right now. I'll do it
another time."*

The entire basketball world didn't have to wait long. In fact,
"another time" came just a month later when Kobe Bryant gave
us one of the greatest performances in the sport's history.

Master at Work: The Performance that Cemented a Legacy

January 22nd, 2006, was a memorable day for basketball.

It was also a special day for Kobe Bryant. For the first time in
her life, Kobe's grandmother wanted to watch Kobe play live as
a Laker. She was incredibly emotional as the game took place
on her late husband's birthday. Kobe's granddad passed away
just two years prior. After the reunion with his grandmother
and reminiscing on the past, Kobe was ready for the game.

Toronto Raptors came to visit.

Ever since ***Vince Carter*** left the Raptors in 04, Toronto was a
mediocre team far away from the play-of-picture. Despite the
lackluster results, they were motivated to grab the win at the
Staples Center. **However, on that January night, motivation
alone couldn't prevent the carnage about to ensue.**

From the opening tip, Toronto made a critical mistake. Years later, while reflecting on this particular game, Bryant said:

> **"After my first bucket, I realized their rotations weren't sharp or early."**

Despite the realization, Toronto took the lead after the first half. Kobe's 27 points didn't help the Lakers, as no one else from the team stepped up to the challenge. Heading into the 3rd quarter, the result on the scoreboard was 63–49 for the Raptors. Coming back from halftime, Kobe immediately got back to work.

He singlehandedly outscored the entire Raptors team in the third quarter. The Lakers took a four-point lead before the fourth and final quarter. By that point, Kobe had 53 points and no intention of stopping. The entire *Staples Center* was on its feet, knowing they were witnessing history in the making.

When the game was on the line, Kobe took over.

Shot after shot, Bryant couldn't miss the target. If he wasn't shooting and making threes, Kobe relied on his iconic jump shot, hitting the basket from various angles.

When the Raptors made changes to prevent baskets from the inside, Kobe would take the ball and splash a three. Or, he would just as easily drive inside for a slam dunk, leaving his defenders helplessly observing.

PERSONAL MASTERY

Whatever the poor Raptors tried, it simply didn't work. On that night, nothing could've possibly worked. Kobe was in the zone.

To make things even worse for Toronto, he didn't show any signs of slowing down. As the game progressed into the final quarter, players were naturally fatigued, which led to a drop in focus and concentration. The Mamba punished every mistake the Raptors made, and he did so viciously.

Bryant moved with a lightning pace throughout the entire game and kept the same intensity for the entire 48 minutes of play.

Just four seconds before the end of the game, Phil Jackson took Kobe out of the game. While he was exiting the floor and heading towards the bench, fans celebrated their hero with an eruption of cheers and applause.

After scoring 28 points in the final quarter, Kobe tallied a record-breaking 81 for the Lakers to win. On that fateful night, Kobe broke two records. In addition to breaking the previous franchise record of 71 set by Elgin Baylor in 1960, Bryant's 81-point game was the second-highest point total in NBA history, surpassed only by Chamberlain's 100-point game in 1962.

That night, another man went down in history as the player who 'allowed' Kobe to score 81 points. The Raptors employed multiple defenders on Bryant, occasionally rotating defenders, yet *Jalen Rose* is remembered as the guy who couldn't stop Kobe.

After a solid career and 13 seasons in the NBA, Jalen became an analyst for ESPN. In 2018, Nike re-released *'The Nike Zoom —*

Kobe 1: Protro,' a line of shoes based on the earliest Nike model Kobe wore during his career. He wore the same model on that January night when he made history.

The occasion provided the ideal opportunity for ESPN and Jalen to catch up with Kobe. Just a few minutes into the interview, Jalen steered the conversation toward the game that marked both of their careers.

> *Jalen: "Before you score that 81, you were breaking all types of records. 40-point games, 60-point games, 60 points in three quarters... So, tell us, what led up to the monster 81-point game?"*

> *Kobe: "Well, it was 1000 makes a day during the summertime. Also, going through things just as I would during the games. I knew exactly what my positions were within the triangle offense. I knew where the shots would be coming from.*

> ***Everything I did through the course of my training was to literally simulate game shots. When I played the game, things were just automatic because I'd already put my body and my mind through that before.***

> *Let me give you an example: sometimes get into the gym for a workout. You on your ball handling and your shooting...But none of that is within a structure and not something you will be doing in the game.*

> *For me, it wasn't like that. **For me, the practice was the***

carbon copy of what I'd be doing in games. By the time season came around, it was just muscle memory."

* * *

Mamba Mentality: The Simple Formula for Mastery

"If you want to be great at something, there is a choice you have to make.

We can all be masters at our craft, but ... there are inherent sacrifices that come along with that — family time, hanging out with your friends, being a great friend, being a great son, or nephew, whatever the case may be.

There are sacrifices that come along with that., the price to pay to be"

In many ways, the Mamba Mentality is synonymous with hard work.

After all, Kobe was the hardest-working player on the team. His philosophy was always to work harder than you think you can work. To reach the level of greatness Bryant aspired to, hard work is unquestioned and non-negotiable.

Yet, there seems to be more to The Mamba Mentality — The Mentality of Greatness than just hard work.

Mamba Mentality is all about striving for excellence, and it's about constant curiosity about the chosen craft. Kobe was driven by the desire to be the best, and he wanted to learn everything he could about the game of basketball.

What made him great and what separated Kobe from other talents of the generation was his attitude. Kobe Bryant was deliberate about his game. The stories about Kobe's workout sessions, intensity, and meticulous approach to basketball are part of the NBA lore, told with the utmost respect by his fellow peers.

In all of those stories, a common theme re-occurs, and it's the one about Kobe's devotion to basketball. From the moment he picked up a ball, Kobe Bryant viewed himself as a life-long learner on a never-ending path to mastery.

Before his masterclass performance and the 81-point game against Toronto, Kobe had to spend years and decades learning and perfecting his craft. *Before he could become a master, Kobe Bryant had to learn how to be a student of the game.*

Throughout his basketball journey, Kobe's teachers were exceptional masters of the game of basketball. He was blessed to be a student of many basketball greats and eager to learn from various legends. While some taught Bryant a specific move to use on the court, others gave him advice or a critique he needed to hear; one **particular man changed Kobe's entire basketball paradigm.**

Throughout his 60 years of coaching, *Tex Winter* became known as one of the most brilliant minds in basketball history.

Tex was renowned as an inventor of the triangle offense, an offensive strategy that has revolutionized the game. After winning more than 450 games in the college ranks, Winter became an assistant coach in the NBA, where he left his greatest legacy. Joining the Chicago Bulls in the late 80s, he brought his patented offense, which Phil Jackson perfected. Together, they created an unstoppable juggernaut in the NBA, winning six NBA titles in the 90s.

Just a few years later, in 1999, Phil joined the Los Angeles Lakers. His old friend and trusted assistant soon followed his steps. In LA, Tex met a brilliant young player with almost limitless potential and a bright future. Kobe Bryant reminded Tex of his former student in Chicago, and he immediately took a liking to the youngster.

As Tex Winter recollected years later, the only noticeable distinction between these two greats was Kobe's curiosity and hunger to learn. The student's enthusiasm certainly inspired the old master, and Tex Winter taught Bryant how to become a true student of the game.

With the utmost respect, Kobe called Tex' *Master Yoda'* and credited him during the talk he gave at *USC Performance Science Institute in 2017:*

> *"The way I was brought up was to pay attention to the detail. Under Phil and Tex Winter, the way we broke down*

> *the film was to the smallest detail.*
>
> *The film we studied was broken down to the right angle, foot placement, timing...It was broken down to looking at the posture of your teammate, looking at how they might feel, and the same thing for the opposition. You are watching the feed at the timeout, looking at how they talk to each other, and taking note of everything you observe.*
>
> *Watching the game for me would take 5 hours, at least. I understand why not many players are willing to do it. I believe that attention to detail and studying the game are missing today.*
>
> *As Tex used to say: 'Everything you need is in the film.''*

From 'Master Yoda,' Kobe learned how to approach the game of basketball with a *'beginner's mind.'* Bryant was fortunate to pick up on this simple yet crucial philosophy any master has to adopt on their journey to greatness.

The beginner's mind, or **Shoshin,** is a concept from Zen Buddhism, and it refers to a student's attitude.

Having a beginner's mind means having an attitude of openness, eagerness, and a lack of preconceptions when studying a subject, even when studying at an advanced level, just as a beginner would. The term is mainly used in the study of Zen Buddhism and Japanese martial arts. It was popularized outside of Japan by Shunryū Suzuki's 1970 book *Zen Mind, Beginner's*

Mind.

The practice of **Shoshin** acts as a counter to the hubris and closed-mindedness often associated with the **Einstellung effect**, where an individual becomes so accustomed to a particular way of doing things that they do not consider or acknowledge new ideas or approaches. *The enemy of any master is the illusion of knowledge, which is the foundation of ignorance.*

Aside from the willingness to commit to a grueling path to mastery, those who embark on this journey need to know that mastery comes with a hefty price.

To be the master, you have to be committed to your craft. You have to seek out knowledge and apply it with vigorous intent. Most importantly, becoming a master requires diligent work.

Master has to do the work, but the nature of the work makes all the difference.

The Practice of a Master

One of the early pioneers in the field of human performance was a Swedish psychologist, **Anders Ericsson**. He was internationally recognized as one of the earliest researchers in the psychological nature of expertise. He studied expert performance in domains such as medicine, music, chess, and sports.

Ericcson was on a mission to discover an answer to a rather simple question: "How do people improve?"

He found that it took around 10,000 hours for people to excel in fields such as chess, golf, and competitive musical performance. Ericcson also found that becoming an expert is not about how much you practice. Rather, it is about **how you practice**.

Anders Ericsson called the concept – **Deliberate Practice.**

It's not a secret that top performers across a wide range of fields: including medicine, music, athletics, writing, and business — use **Deliberate Practice** to attain and maintain expertise, and eventually, with enough commitment and dedication, those special few practitioners may venture into the land of mastery.

Being the absolute best requires doing differently than the rest.

While regular practice might include mindless repetitions, deliberate practice requires focused attention and is conducted with the **specific goal of improving performance.** In other words, those seeking mastery must commit to a long journey of purposeful and systematic practice.

Throughout his entire 20-year career, Kobe Bryant has been nothing but purposeful and systematic in his approach. Kobe deliberately practiced within the structure of the game.

Bryant always practiced at game speed. He wouldn't just shoot 1,000 shots alone in a gym. He'd shoot each of those shots while mentally pushing himself to move and react as though defenders were running toward him, and he had a fraction of a second to release the ball.

PERSONAL MASTERY

Kobe had a goal for each and every workout session. Whether it was a shooting session where the goal was to hit a thousand' game shots' or conditioning training where the goal was building endurance by running,

Kobe had a purpose behind his training methodology. Each and every workout session required unparalleled toughness and focus.

Kobe Bryant used to pick a spot on the court that he knew he could reach in two dribbles, and he'd use all of his might and speed to get there as quickly as possible. He knew where he was going, but the defender wouldn't. It's something he practiced over and over again in dimly lit gyms in the early hours of the day.

Come game time, the mastery was effortless.

Fundamentals: The Secret to Winning and Success

Over the years, and after his playing career, less-known details about his workout regimens and routines emerged to the wider public. One of those details includes his obsessiveness with 'basic' basketball drills. Kobe would work on the basic footwork and offensive moves for a full hour before doing anything else for that training day.

Dwayne Wade, the Miami Heat and NBA Legend, once said he watched Bryant warm up for the upcoming game. He was impressed, mesmerized, and baffled at the same time. Before the game, for 20 minutes, Kobe was making the same move over and over again, a basic drill Wade described as: 'Left foot dribble, pull up and shot.'

Unsurprisingly, Kobe used the same move to score 40 on the 'Heat' that night. They knew what he would do, yet there was no chance of stopping him.

The greatest testament to his mastery and fundamentals came in his last-ever performance against the Utah Jazz on April 13th, 2016. In his home, the *Staples Center*, Kobe Bryant scored 60 points in a narrow 101–96 Lakers win. He saved the best for last with arguably the greatest farewell performance in the history of sports.

None of the sixty Bryant poured on the Jazz that night came from a flashy dunk or any other high-flying move. Once revered as a phenom in the air, Kobe's physicality and athleticism were far and long gone. As he matured, his game naturally evolved until he reached its final stage — Mastery.

In fact, his last ever game was a masterclass, and Kobe taught the lesson of basketball fundamentals.

Masters never get bored with basics. That is why they are masters.
In 2007, after ten grueling seasons in the NBA, Kobe's knees began to swell and hurt more than usual. The physicality of the game at the highest level took its toll on Bryant. His goal was to play at the highest level for another ten years, but he knew he needed a different approach to training and recovery regimen.

Always the student of the game, Kobe reached out to Michael

Jordan for advice. MJ dealt with similar problems during the latter half of his career. During his playing days, Michael was notorious for keeping his methods and secrets to himself, but when Kobe reached out, Jordan gracefully pointed him toward *Tim Grover.*

Tim Grover is an iconic figure in the world of the NBA, and he is the man indirectly responsible for the Chicago Bulls' domination in the 90s. As the strength, conditioning, and high-performance coach, he helped MJ transform his body and, in the process, elevate his game to another stratosphere.

After working with Michael Jordan, Tim Grover worked with Kobe for the next few years. During those years, he spent a lot of time with Bryant and got to know Kobe, the man behind the NBA legend.

In his bestselling book, **'Winning,'** Tim gave us valuable insight into the mind of Kobe Bryant, his practice routine, and his devotion to the fundamentals of the game.

> *"The greatest player in the world, working on a basic chest pass. Why? Routine. Basics. Fundamentals. The court was his battlefield, and he knew where all the mines were planted.*
>
> ***If you can't master the fundamentals, you can't master anything else.***
>
> *Even before games, in the tunnel, he would go through*

the motion of a chest pass, watching an imaginary ball release perfectly off his fingers and thumbs, spinning its way through his mind, cutting through the unnecessary thoughts in his head.

His fundamentals were so well rehearsed. He never had to think about those basics during a game. He knew if he could get to a certain spot on the court, nothing could stop him. Most players have a spot like that. MJ had them all over the floor; that was his minefield. He knew exactly where to position himself and where his doomed opponents would be blown up.

Mamba mentality is about dedication to the craft of choice. Kobe loved basketball, and as much as he improved as a player, he was still a life-long learner on the quest to become the best. *Kobe Bryant propelled himself to the land of masters with a purposeful, systematic approach to the game of basketball.*

* * *

From Zero to Hero: The Genesis of The Mamba Mentality & The Essence of Mastery

The major misconception about Kobe's career accomplishments has to be one about the role of his natural talent. To be fair, talent, in general, is widely misunderstood, especially in relation to success in life. Talent is not a god-given ability or a superpower reserved for a special few. It is merely a natural inclination towards certain activities.

Talent is undoubtedly an inherent gift, but one we have to discover and develop as we go through life. Kobe was fortunate to find his gift when he fell in love with basketball at age 3.

By the time he was old enough to play with others, he was the best. He relied on his natural talent while playing in Italy, but when he returned to the USA for the summer league, **Kobe was in for a rude awakening.**

In the Summer of 1990, Aged 12, Kobe Bryant played the entire summer league without scoring a single point. Not from a free throw, breakaway layup, or even an open shot. Not even a lucky shot.

Unlike his peers from Italy, kids in America were bigger, stronger, faster, and more athletic than Kobe.

Adding to the misery was the fact that *Sonny Hill League* was a prominent junior league in Philadelphia, where both his father and uncle had much success. After the last game of the season, his father gave little Kobe all the comfort he needed. Joe told his son that regardless of the outcome, he would always be loved. He encouraged his son to dream big and work even harder, which is advice Kobe took to heart.

From that moment, he developed a plan for getting better. He devised a strategy for development. Young Kobe realized the importance of long-term strategic planning.

He knew he wouldn't catch up with those kids in a week, month, or even a year. He deliberately focused on a particular aspect of the game and obsessively worked on it. He accessed his game and evaluated his skills, then prioritized those skills for a few months until he could do them automatically without conscious effort.

The following season, when he came back, he was better, and improvement was obvious. It was evident that his deliberate practice led to his incredible development.

At this point, Kobe Bryant was a well-rounded player with no glaring weakness in his game. Seeing the results paying off, Kobe doubled down on the hard work, but he also focused on strategically developing his weaknesses. In fact, Kobe forced himself to play to his weaknesses instead of relying on his strengths just to win games.

The season after, 14-year-old Kobe was undoubtedly the best player in the *Sunny Hill Junior League.* The same kids that used to intimidate and bully Kobe were now completely helpless.

On the basketball court, they were left at his mercy. Kobe had none. He dominated and demolished anyone who stood in front. Unable to do anything to stop him, all they could do was witness his ascension. To make things even worse for other kids, Kobe finally grew into his frame. Now standing at 6ft1, Bryant was no longer a short, scrawny kid, and he no longer needed big padded knee braces to protect his fragile and hurting knees.

In just two short years, Kobe Bryant went from a boy with zero points to the status of the best player in the state of Pennsylvania. The great *Wilt Chamberlain* once held the same honor, and this recognition gave young Kobe all the necessary momentum to keep going.

Years later, in an interview with **Lewis Howes**, he revealed the 'secret' of his insane early development. It turned out that there was no secret, as **everything Kobe did was methodical, practical, and, most importantly, purposeful. The rest was up to Mother Nature and Father Time to provide.**

He trained more than any other player, and he trained deliberately.

> *"It happened in two years. I wasn't expecting it to happen, but it did...Because what I had to work on was the basics and the fundamentals while they relied on their athleticism and natural ability.*
>
> *Because I stick with the fundamentals, it's just caught up to them.*
>
> *My knees stopped hurting; I grew into my frame, and..."*

Bryant wished to leave the sentence unfinished and let it linger in the listener's thoughts. Still, Lewis perfectly summarized the story of the origins of the Mamba Mentality and the essence of Personal Mastery.

> *'Once you have the fundamentals, the hard work, the mentality, and you add the athleticism to the mix...Then it's game over.'*

4

The Identity & The Role of Alter-Ego

> *"The mamba himself is a character that helped me get into the character needed to win on the basketball court. There is a difference between Kobe as a person and Kobe as a player. I can be a Mambo–Jambo daddy and a teddy bear at home, but I gotta lock in when I step into the staples center. It became about the philosophy of life, about being present."*

During the mid to late 80s, the boxing world saw the meteoric rise of Mike Tyson. At the tender age of 20, Tyson won the WBC (World Boxing Council) heavyweight title in 1986, becoming the youngest boxer in history to do so.

Shortly thereafter, Tyson won the WBA (World Boxing Association) heavyweight title, followed by a title in the IBF (International Boxing Federation), thus uniting all of his tiles to become the undisputed champion.

For the next three years, he held and defended a championship. Tyson would easily and quickly dispatch any challenger who dared to step into the ring. He was ruthless and vicious, and he wanted to hurt the opponent. One highlight knockout after another, Mike Tyson would separate his opponents from consciousness time and time again.

Rightfully considered the greatest boxer in the world by his peers and fans, the media gave him a fitting nickname — **The Iron Mike.**

But for Mike Tyson, "The Iron Mike" wasn't just a nickname. For Mike Tyson, "The Iron Mike" was an entirely different persona. The Iron Mike was Tyson's alter ego, his second self.

Iron Mike was the total opposite of Mike Tyson. He was fearless and feared at the same time. He would terrify and break his enemies before the opening bell. He was everything Mike Tyson desired to be growing up. Despite the well-deserved reputation of the '*Baddest Man on the Planet,*' Tyson was far from invincible.

Growing up in various high-crime ghetto neighborhoods, he lived in constant fear. Until he retaliated the first time, little Mike was regularly bullied and ridiculed for his high-pitched voice and his lisp. He got into fights and troubles with the law, and by the age of 13, Mike Tyson was arrested 38 times.

When he was only 16, his prostitute mother passed away, leaving him in the care of a complete stranger. Fortunately for her, for Mike, and for the rest of the world, that stranger was none other than *Cuss D'amato.* Legendary boxing coach recognized a gift Mike had buried deep inside him. Cuss was a father figure and a legal guardian for the youngster, and he helped develop his talent.

Despite the aggression and violent outbursts, Little Mike was afraid, and more often than not, Little Mike was confused. He needed guidance and a mentor, which is what he got in the D'amato.

When he took in Mike Tyson, Cuss D'amato was an old and wise man. He saw through the rough exterior and recognized a scared boy cowering in fear. He also recognized another figure in the darkest corners of his young protege's soul - The one with the spirit of a warrior, thirsty for violence and victory.

Cuss was the one who encouraged Mike to find and channel his inner warrior, who later became one of the greatest heavy-weight boxers of all time, known as 'The Iron Mike.'

The idea of an alter ego is far from a novelty.
It's been around almost for as long as recorded history. Back in the early days, right before Jesus was born, another Great man known as **Marcus Tullius Cicero** made the first recorded notion of the alter ego, or the second self. He coined the term **alter-ego** and described it as a '**second self, a trusted friend.**'

The existence of "another self" was first fully recognized in the 18th century, when **Anton Mesmer,** a German physician and astronomer, and his followers used hypnosis to separate the alter ego. These experiments showed a behavior pattern that was distinct from the personality of the individual when they were in the waking state compared with when they were under hypnosis. Effectively, another character had developed in the altered state of consciousness but in the same body.

The existence of the alter ego has been well documented and confirmed in many Greats from all walks of life.

Indeed, almost all of the greatest performers from various fields had an alter ego, a second self, a character that serves a particular purpose. Those who transcended their respective industries are especially known for having an alter ego and, sometimes, multiple ones.

For Beyonce, that character is Sacha Fierce.
Beyonce was naturally shy and reserved, and she struggled with self-confidence and anxiety issues for many years. In the world of show business, talents are required to perform, and for many, that requirement creates enormous pressure. Beyonce found a way to deal with stress and thrive in the music industry once she created an alter ego. Before stepping up to the stage to perform in front of tens of thousands of screaming fans, *Sacha Fierce appears and takes over the show.*

David Bowie portrayed numerous characters throughout his career, but **Ziggy Stardust** is his definitive alter-ego. Conceived right at the start of his glamorous career, Ziggy was an omnisexual alien rock star sent to Earth as a messenger of hope, peace, and love. The character influenced the entire generation and changed the music forever. *The success of the character and its iconic look catapulted Bowie into international superstardom.*

Oftentimes, if not always, alter-egos emerge from a dire situation.

In 1996, a commercial and critical flop of his first album, '*Infinite,*' in combination with his tumultuous personal life, brought **Eminem** to the brink of suicide. He was at the lowest point in his life, and he had to change and evolve. In his particular case, the evolution came once he unleashed his suppressed emotions in the form of an alter-ego.

***Slim Shady**, a sadistic, violent, yet hilariously witty character, took the music scene by storm and catapulted Eminem **(real and birth name Marshall Matters)** to immediate stardom.*

Interestingly, an alter ego doesn't always have to be a 'real' person. For some, it's an animal.

For one particular man, his alter-ego was a snake.

* * *

The Deadliest Predator in The World

In Africa, there are four species of mamba. Three of them are green, beautiful, and deadly. The fourth is aggressive, fast, and vicious and is known as the Black Mamba.

Although their natural color is dark gray, this mamba is named after the pitch-black insides of its wide-open jaw. Illusive in appearance, deadly in their essence.

THE IDENTITY & THE ROLE OF ALTER-EGO

One of the world's most lethal snakes, the Black Mamba, has quite a reputation. It is the fastest land snake in the world. It is the longest species of venomous snake in Africa and the second longest in the world. Mamba can grow to up to 14 feet and is an equally efficient killer on the ground, in trees, and in water.

Their venom kills in a matter of minutes, and although the antidote exists, it's not widely available in mamba's natural habitat — Sub-Saharan Africa, region of Africa. Being so infamous and terrifying, Black Mamba got into the lore and legend of local inhabitants.

Black Mamba's notorious bite makes even creatures several hundred times bigger stay away. One bite from the mamba can kill fifteen grown men. The toxins in mamba's venom attach to the chemical receptors of the victim and block communication between nerves and muscles. The result is a rather quick and painful death.

> **"The mamba can strike with 99% accuracy at maximum speed, in rapid succession. That's the kind of basketball precision I want to have."**
> **— Kobe Bryant on the premise of the Black Mamba Alter-ego.**

Understanding where the Black Mamba character came from requires understanding the context of its inception. **The dreadful circumstances of Kobe's personal life served as the catalyst for the emergence of The Black Mamba.**

In hindsight, the single incident in July of 2003 sent Kobe down the path of self-discovery and self-recreation. The version of Kobe Bryant that emerged on the other side of the storm is a testament to his legacy of greatness. It is also a testimony of the role Kobe's identity and alter-ego played during the darkest times of his life.

* * *

Recreate Yourself and Forge Your Greatest Destiny

2003 was the best year in Kobe's life. It was also the worst year in Kobe's life.

In just 12 months, Bryant experienced the dichotomy of life, with all the blessings on the one side and all the cruelty and unfairness on the other.

By the early summer, Kobe Bryant was at the top of the world. His lovely wife, Vannesa, just gave birth to their first child, a baby daughter named Natalia. The baby brought the family together. For the past few years, Kobe had disagreements with his mother and father. Pamela and Joe Bryant disapproved of Kobe's marriage for several reasons, believing them to be too young for such an important step. None of that mattered once Natalia was born. The family was finally united and together again.

On the court, Kobe's 2002/2003 season marked another leap straight to the top echelon of the NBA. Posting the best numbers of his career with 30 points, six rebounds, seven assists, and more than two steals per game, Kobe Bryant finished 3rd in the MVP voting. He cemented his place in both

'All-NBA' and *'All-Defensive'* first teams, proving his reputation as the best guard since Michael Jordan.

Despite Kobe's impressive season, the Lakers ultimately fell short in the playoffs. After a hard-fought series, the **San Antonio Spurs** defeated the Lakers in the Western Conference semifinal. The final result 4–2 paints a vastly different picture from the action on the court. Each game of the series was tightly contested, but ultimately, San Antonio prevailed and went on to win the NBA Championship.

The Lakers made major additions to the squad by adding 'All-Star' power in the forms of veterans **Karl Malone** and **Garry Payton**. LA was ready for another push at the title, and they were considered heavy favorites before the 2004 season. The starting lineup of **Garry Payton**, **Karl Malone**, **Shaquille O'Neal**, and **Kobe Bryant** was led from the bench by the most successful coach in NBA history, **Phil Jackson.**

At that point in time, there wasn't a team in the league that could stop this version of the LA Lakers. Indeed, it seemed as if only the powers that be or the basketball gods could prevent the Lakers from winning 4th championship in five years.

The season was hampered by injuries to all of the major stars at the decisive points during the campaign.

The starting lineup of Shaq, Kobe, Karl, and Gary played only 11 games together during the regular season. The downfall started before the season began, with the initial incident serving as the first domino to fall, setting an entire chain of events in effect.

In July 2003, the world was struck with the shocking news that Kobe Bryant was accused of rape. He denied the accusations, stating that the sexual act with an accuser was consensual. Yet, the damage was done.

Overnight, Kobe's once impeccable reputation was tarnished by the accusation. Seemingly, out of nowhere, private records from his interview with the investigators appeared in public.

The media did their best to get the most out of the situation. Yesterday's hero was now the villain hanging on the wall of shame. With each new 'exclusive update,' they played a part in shaping the public's opinion of Kobe Bryant. Before the trial even started, he was portrayed as guilty. Through carefully crafted narratives, most mainstream media and news outlets did their best to paint Bryant as an abuser.

Everywhere the Lakers went, the spotlight was on Kobe. Some fans made sure to let him know how much they hated him as they heavily booed and screamed all kinds of profanities.

His previously spotless reputation and 'clean image' were under a major threat. All of his sponsors and partners decided to turn their back on him as soon as the allegations came to light. (The only exception was **NIKE**, who stood by Kobe, which was a gesture he remembered and appreciated for the rest of his life.)

Worst of all, Kobe's actions would end up hurting those he loved the most.

He made the mistake of adultery. That mistake would cause so much pain for the family, which was on the brink of falling apart. Understandably, his wife Vanessa was heartbroken. Yet, she decided to forgive Kobe for the adultery and stand beside her husband. Despite the forgiveness, trust can hardly be restored once broken, and the two began a long journey to repair their marriage.

Vanessa believed Kobe was innocent and didn't let her husband face accusations and scrutiny alone. However, their marriage was on shaky grounds. Their relationship was strained and stressful, and the lack of privacy and space given by the public certainly didn't help.

> *"Going through these dark times made me ask a lot of questions and realize what is important in life.*
>
> *Everything I considered significant, the championships and endorsements, wasn't the most important thing. I lost sight of what is the most important thing in the world — Family.*
>
> *It's the man's job to protect his family, and to look out for his family. It's the man's job always to be the anchor of stability for the family...In that aspect, I failed miserably."*
>
> *— Kobe Bryant, reflecting on his darkest days.*

As hard as it was, with the entire world watching closely, Bryant owned up to his mistake and took responsibility for his actions. He refused the role of a victim of circumstances. In his mind, he had something much bigger to fight for.

With his family falling apart in front of his eyes, he did the only thing he could. Kobe fought for his family, freedom, and justice. By the end of 2003, his future surely looked uncertain and bleak. Life as he knew it could end as soon as the verdict was reached. For Bryant, the worst part was the constant state of suspense, waiting for the end of an ordeal.

One of the most memorable yet unreported stories of Kobe's greatness has to be the one from the 2003/2004 Lakers season, collectively dubbed as 'The Last Chance.' Despite the outcome of the season, the way he handled being a Laker is admirable. Even the most prominent critics and outright haters had to admit Kobe's professionalism and his impeccable behavior on and off the court.

Before the 2004 season, Phil Jackson tried to reach Kobe multiple times, never to receive a callback. Together with Lakers general manager *Mitch Kupchak*, Jackson considered offering Kobe a leave of absence to deal with the upcoming trial. The Los Angeles Lakers management fully, and maybe rightfully, expected Kobe to sit out the following season. They planned to give him all the time and space he needed to deal with the off-court issues and contribute to the team in any way he could.

A few weeks before the 2003/2004 season, Bryant reached out to Phil and the rest of the board with an explicit desire to collectively treat this season as any other. Any other athlete in that situation would take a few months or even the entire season off to focus on the trial.

Any other but Kobe Bryant.

He was flying back and forth in his private charter to Colorado to appear in court, and he tried his best not to miss too many games that season. He would spend a day in court in Colorado, fly back to LA, and on the way to the game, he would warm up by riding a stationary bike in the back of a van that transported him to the arena.

More than once, he would show up five minutes before the game, forcing the Lakers to make quick changes and adjustments. From the first day of the season, no one could question Kobe's commitment to the team and their cause of winning a championship.

Since the season's opening day, one thing has been crystal clear. ***Come hell or high water, Kobe Bryant was going to show up.***

He wanted to play and needed to play because the game of basketball was his only form of escapism. Since his earliest days in Italy, the game was his refuge from the harsh realities of life. He knew that no matter what happened around him, he could always turn to basketball.

The Black Mamba: The Character that Changed the Landscape of the Game

Somehow, during the early part of the season, Kobe was different. His trademark focus and intensity were absent from his usual game. Considering all the circumstances, one could hardly blame him. However, the root cause of the issue lay much deeper than losing a ball in transition or missing an open shot.

For Bryant, the game of basketball was the only sacred place, and now, it was invaded and violated by external noise. He felt like a drowning man trying to catch a breath before the next wave inevitably comes tumbling and crashing from above.

Kobe didn't enjoy the game like he used to. His mind was preoccupied with a myriad of other pressing and urgent matters outside of the court.

During that time, he had a lot of sleepless nights. During one particular night, turning into the early morning, Kobe couldn't turn off his racing mind and looked for any possible distraction. He turned on the TV and stumbled upon a nature documentary.

The movie was about the deadliest predators in the world, and right at the top of that list was a fierce reptile. The snake is known as the black mamba. Kobe was drawn to this creature, and right then and there, he realized what he had to do.

To regain his slipping sense of control, Kobe had to separate Kobe Bryant, the man, and Kobe Bryant, the player.

Kobe, the man, deals with the aftermath of his life choice. Off the court, he fights for his freedom and for his family, who is going through the darkest times. The trial was set to start later in 2003, and if found guilty, Kobe faced probation to a life sentence in prison.

Kobe, the basketball player, deals with the game and everything that happens on the wooden court. Bryant knew that on the court, he had to be zoned in, hyper-alert, and his usual self. Yet, Kobe didn't want to be his old, usual self.

No.

He wanted to go a step further and elevate his game to yet another level. To do so, Kobe knew he had to be deadly, vicious, and efficient, just like ***The Black Mamba.***

> *"I went from a person who was at the top of his game and had everything to a year later, having absolutely no idea where life is going or if you are even going to be a part of life as we all know it.*
>
> *I had to separate myself. It felt like there were so many things coming at once. It was just becoming very, very confusing. I had to organize and compartmentalize things.*
>
> *So I created "The Black Mamba."*
>
> *Kobe deals with life outside of the court. The Black Mamba steps on the court and does what he does." —* Kobe Bryant on the character of The Black Mamba

The boos and chants of screaming fans didn't disappear overnight. On the contrary, Kobe's reception in arenas outside of LA got much worse before it got any better. They were louder, meaner, and nastier than ever, poking the wounds and rubbing salt on them.

Many fans at the time would constantly find new, clever ways to provoke Bryant. Whether with a new chant to yell at Kobe during games or with handmade large paper signs and banners, the fans aimed to destabilize and throw him off his game.

At first, they managed to get inside his head as everything was simply too hectic for Bryant to deal with. The mounting pressure, pending trial, family issues, and all the surrounding noise proved difficult to handle. Despite going through personal hell, Kobe also recovered from a nagging knee injury for the most part of the preseason.

However, as the season progressed, the 'new version' of Kobe took shape in front of our eyes. Game after game, he showed up and delivered a performance, usually in the clutch moments of the game. Despite the entire year of trial, injuries, and misfortunes, the 'new' Kobe was at the point where nothing could affect his game. On the court, Bryant fully immersed himself in the mamba character.

Just like any other great performer, before heading to the stage, he dedicated pre-game rituals and routines to channel his emotions and get into the character, ready for another clinical performance.

Bryant would sit in solitude, visualizing himself as the Black Mamba Character. He mentally rehearsed his actions on the court, whether it was a defensive or offensive play.

Years later, in a conversation with a famous talk-show host, **Jimmy Kimmel**, Kobe admitted to drawing inspiration from **Michael Myers,** the mask-wearing villain and the main antagonist from the 'Halloween' series of slasher movies. In particular, he was attracted to the blank and emotionless look of the character and his menacing presence.

Kobe believed one critical factor led to the rise of his game. Through the alter-ego that is The Black Mamba, he effectively found an outlet for all the dark emotions he had been suppressing for a long time. He transferred all of his pent-up anger, rage, and frustration onto the basketball court.

The Black Mamba could act on the rage and aggression that Kobe, the man, felt. As the Black Mamba, Kobe Bryant played the game of basketball with unprecedented ferocity and anger. Anyone who would try to stand in his way would get demolished by the avalanche of rage.

Through sheer determination against all odds, in the 2003/2004 season, the LA Lakers were in title contention, mostly due to Kobe's heroics on the court.

Once again, he surprised the entire basketball globe with yet another step up in his game, once again proving he is one of the best players in the league. Bryant was selected to the All-NBA first team for a third straight year. He was also selected for the All-NBA first defensive team, proving his immense value on both ends of the floor.

What he did during the 2003/2004 season, during the year when he fought for his freedom and his life, is quite simply remarkable. In a situation where any athlete would take time off and focus on the extensive and exhausting trial, Kobe proved once again that he was no ordinary man.

Flying from LA to Colorado and back on a regular basis, fighting for justice and his freedom, fighting to keep his family together, and leading his team to the NBA finals is a remarkable feat and a testament to the power of the human spirit.

Phil Jackson, a man who witnessed Bryant's growth and evolution for more than a decade, summarized Bryant's incredible achievement:

> *"No professional athlete, I believe, has tried to perform at the top level of his sport for any extended period of time while fighting to keep his freedom. How Kobe manages to compartmentalize is beyond me."*

Indeed, no other athlete before or since has managed to pull a similar feat. The 'secret' to Kobe's incredible ability to compartmentalize, to separate personal from professional, has to be correlated to his unique ability to bring forth his alter-ego, **The Black Mamba.**

The Aftermath of a Dreadful Season: Kobe's Trial & Reputation, and The Evolution of Black Mamba Character

Bryant's heroics throughout the year and in the playoffs were nothing short of spectacular.

Remarkably, as the long and grueling campaign was coming to an end and by the playoff, Kobe elevated his individual performances. He singlehandedly carried the Lakers through the end of a regular season, securing a second seed in the Western Conference.

In the 2004 playoffs, The Black Mamba was almost unstoppable. In a super team consisting of three other future Hall of Famers, including Shaq, Karl Malone, and Garry Payton, *Kobe Bryant was the undisputed leader on the court.* They've managed to reach the NBA Finals, where they were upset by the **Detroit Pistons,** who won the series in five games.

Unfortunately, the star-filled Lakers squad ultimately failed to win the championship. Winning the title, their 4th in just five years would cement their place in the pantheon of the greatest basketball dynasties that ever existed.

Losing in the finals signalized a new era for the Lakers as Shaquille O'Neal and Phil Jackson left the organization in the summer of 04. (Although the 'Zen-Master' returned the following year and won two more championships by the end of the decade)

The inevitable question almost imposes itself:
What was the aftermath of an unprecedented season in sports

history?

The Lakers organization was stuck between a rock and a hard place.
They had to make a tough call. The tension within the team has reached a critical point. It was evident that Shaq and Kobe couldn't coexist anymore. The man at the helm, Phil Jackson, sided with the big man. He outright refused to come back the next season if Kobe Bryant was still part of the team.

The Lakers' management traded Shaquille O'Neal to Miami and refused to extend Phil's contract. Instead, they've signed a new 7-year $136 million dollar deal with Kobe Bryant, making him the De-Facto leader of the Los Angeles Lakers.

Kobe Bryant was acquitted of all charges on September 1st, 2004. After 14 months of living on the edge and going through personal hell, Eagle County District Judge dismissed the charges against Bryant after prosecutors spent more than $200,000 preparing for trial because his accuser informed them that she was unwilling to testify.

However, the accuser filed a civil lawsuit against Bryant just a month prior, and the two-party settled out of court. The two sides reached an agreement in March of 2005, and a reported settlement was more than $2.5 million. Despite the verdict of innocence, Kobe's reputation and image were tainted.

The entire ordeal deeply shook Bryant. Although reluctant to talk about this particular part of his life, he admitted how the criminal charges changed him. The journey of redemption was long, but he eventually made it to the top of the mountain. Kobe became one of the greatest players of all time, an NBA icon, and a role model for future generations. Over time, and despite a few rocky patches on the road, Kobe and Vannesa stayed together until the end, and she gave him three more precious daughters. Their love stood the test of time.

The Black Mamba character evolved as Kobe matured and eventually served its purpose. The alter ego elevated Kobe's game, and over time, the character morphed into a new version that reflected his overall game. We, the fans, will forever remember the year of the Black Mamba in the history of the game.

In the season where stakes were much higher than 'just' basketball, Kobe Bryant showed up. *The fond memory of that version of Kobe, the alter-ego known as* **The Black Mamba,** *lives in the minds and hearts of Kobe's fans.*

5

Uncompromising Integrity

> *"You have to be true to who you are."*

June 15, 2001, was a historic day for NBA basketball.
The Lakers won their second championship in a row, winning against the Philadelphia 76ers on their home court. Throughout the 2001 NBA playoff, the LA Lakers lost only one game. They made history while demonstrating unseen dominance in the process.

June 15, 2001, was a special day for Kobe Bryant.
Within a few short years, he became one of the best players in the league. In a season where he averaged 28 points, and together with *Shaquille O'Neal*, he just led the Lakers to back-to-back championships. 22-year-old Kobe forever etched his name in basketball history by winning his second NBA championship in his hometown of Philadelphia.

Kobe Bryant was at the top of the basketball world; he had just won the NBA championship in his hometown, yet something was missing. *During the celebration in the locker room, Kobe was seen crying on camera, and the word soon got through about the reason.*

His mom and dad weren't there to watch him play and see him win.

The Bryants were noticeably absent from the entire series with the 76ers and were absent throughout the regular season. Although Kobe knew they wouldn't be there, he secretly hoped they would.

Bryant wanted to win the title for his father, who played in the same arena many decades earlier. Joe was more than Philadelphia's player. He was Philly's hometown hero. Although Kobe himself was never as embraced by the city as his dad was, he wanted to make his dad proud once again in a place they considered a home not too long ago.

As much as it hurt him at the time, he knew there was no other way. Put in front of an ultimatum, Kobe Bryant made a difficult decision, and now he had to live with it.

During the 2000/2001 NBA Season, the media dedicated much time and resources to the private life of Kobe Bryant. Not surprisingly, considering his status in the league and the dominant fashion in which the Lakers cruised to their second title. One of the prevailing narratives the media shaped and told during the year was the one of Kobe's fallout with his family.

In a highly publicized feud, Pamela and Joe were unsupportive of Kobe's life choices. Most notably, the parents disapproved of his marriage to Vanessa Laine, believing him to be too young and inexperienced to make such a mature, critical decision. Reportedly, one of the main issues was the fact that Vanessa comes from a different heritage.

Both Pamela and Joe shared a personal conviction that Kobe's wife must be from the African-American community. For a short while, Bryant was torn between his two families. The one who brought him up to this world and the one he started with a woman he chose and the woman he loved.

Eventually, Kobe had to make a hard choice, and he did when he married Vannessa on April 18, 2001. Out of protest, his parents and siblings didn't attend the wedding. Although he hoped they might show up for the final game in their hometown, Kobe knew his dad wasn't there to share the moment with his son.

Yet, his wife, Vanessa Bryant, was there to share the moment of glory with her husband. Since the day they met, she has been Kobe's number-one fan and supporter. In his post-finals interview, Bryant credited Vanessa for supporting him on his journey to greatness.

For Kobe Bryant, there was only one thing in life more important than basketball. The only thing that carried more weight for Kobe was his family. Despite choosing to turn their back on their son and brother, and regardless of the public feud, Kobe still supported them wholeheartedly. Even though they refused to speak to him for more than two years, Bryant continued giving and providing for his mother, father, and sisters.

He kept giving material riches and all the other luxuries the NBA superstar could afford until he learned a lesson the hard way.

He falsely believed he was providing for his family, but in reality, all he did was make his family, mostly his sisters, dependent on him. He realized he was robbing them of opportunities to grow and become the best version of themselves. Kobe wanted to see his sisters without a care in the world, but he realized he denied them the most precious gifts life could offer: *Independence and Growth.*

As hard as it was, Kobe had to make a difficult decision. The only decision aligned with his integrity. He stopped spoiling his sisters, and he allowed them to face the world on their own. He believed that was the only way for his sisters to succeed, and he was right. Ultimately, both *Sharia and Shaya grew up to be successful in their careers and personal lives.*

Throughout his entire life, one thing was crystal clear. Kobe Bryant was a man who always stood up for what he believed in. He was a man driven by his personal beliefs and convictions. He lived in accordance with his personal integrity.

Nathaniel Branden, a well-known psychotherapist, a doctor in psychology, and certainly the expert in the matter, defined personal integrity as: **"Integration of ideals, convictions, standards, beliefs, and behavior. When our behavior is congruent with our professed values, and when ideals and practice match up, we have Personal Integrity".**

Numerous stories from various sources paint Bryant as a man with a specific code of conduct. All of those stories add to Kobe's mystique, and they are a testament to his ultimate greatness.

One man named **Samaki Walker** felt firsthand just how deep Bryant's personal convictions truly were. In February 2002, during the Lakers' historic run, *Kobe Bryant slapped Walker over $100 dollars.*

Samaki was Kobe's teammate and a part of the Lakers squad that dominated the NBA in the early 2000s. During those years, the team had a game they would usually play at the end of the practice called 'Half-Court Shot Game.' The entire team would put in $100 dollars in the pot, and the first player to hit the shot from the half-court would win the contest and take all the money from the pot.

As usual, Kobe won. A day later, Kobe came to collect the money.

Apparently, Samaki Walker had no intention of paying what he owed. According to some reports, he even rudely dismissed Kobe's request. Before Samaki could process the confrontation that just occurred and possibly reevaluate his decision not to pay, *Kobe smacked him right across the forehead.*

All hell broke loose as the two giants scuffled before being pulled away from each other by teammates. To make the incident more frightening was the fact the fight happened on a team bus during the ride to the game. The pair quickly resolved the matter, and the team proceeded on its winning ways, clinching another title in 2002.

Regardless, on that particular day and on that particular bus ride, Samaki Walker learned just how far Kobe was willing to go over the matter of principles.

Kobe knew he had made a hasty decision in the heat of the moment, reacting instinctively. The younger version of Kobe was much more hot-headed, to the point where cheap shots were allowed and justified. As he calmed down, Bryant owned up to his mistake and apologized.

Over the years, naturally, Kobe Bryant evolved. Yet, his fundamental beliefs remained unchanged and were even fortified by his maturation, experience, and, ultimately, wisdom.

It's not a secret that he hated losing, but he accepted it as part of the game. What Kobe Bryant despised was the lack of effort and commitment to the cause. Until the final day of his career, he sacrificed everything to win for the Lakers. *During the final few seasons of his career, Kobe played with a younger generation utterly void of any desire to win.*

In 2015, his LA teammates faced Kobe's wrath after a blowout defeat to Portland. It was far from the only one that season, but in this particular game, The Lakers didn't even try. Due to the injury, Bryant was on the bench, which he left early due to dismal performance by his teammates.

Luckily for them, this older and wiser version of Kobe didn't resort to throwing strikes and cheap shots. He waited for the team to gather in the dressing room, not saying a word. Once the entire team was in the locker room, he gave them a treatment and attitude adjuster.

According to **Nick Young,** his teammate for those final few years, Bryant questioned their collective spirit and individual character before proceeding to tell them to take their shoes off. Fascinatingly, the entire Lakers team wore Kobe's signature Nike sneakers. (Except for only two players who wore different brands.)

With a blank stare and a lack of any facial expression, Kobe wasn't playing around. Terrified of his look, Nick and the rest of the squad took 'his' shoes off and waited for further instructions. Nick Young recalls the incident which became well known as *"The Shoe Story"*:

> "Kobe made us throw our shoes, well 'his' shoes, to the trash. He told us we were playing like trash and didn't deserve to wear his shoes. He said that no one gets to wear his shoes until we improve as a team and show a desire to win."

Coincidentally, another story of Kobe's fundamental beliefs is deeply intertwined with footwear. Behind the fiasco story of Kobe vs. Adidas lays one of the most notable examples of Kobe's integrity. Not willing to compromise on what he believed was right, Bryant paid $8 million dollars to be released from the contract.

The German multinational sports company Adidas signed Kobe

Bryant as a teenager straight from Lower Marion High School on a 6-year deal worth approximately $48 million dollars. At the time, it seemed the match was made in heaven. However, as time went on, the business relationship went sour.

The two sides couldn't seem to agree on the design of the sneakers, both from the functionality and the aesthetic standpoint. The final nail in this turbulent relationship was the release of the infamous "Adidas Kobe 2."

The company was more interested in the looks and the design of the shoe. They reportedly rejected numerous of Kobe's input and feedback. Instead, their lead designer, **Eirik Lund Nielsen**, looked elsewhere for inspiration. In a somewhat baffling decision, he turned to the automotive industry, specifically the **Audi TT Roadster**, as the base shape of the sneaker.

Prior to its release in December 2001, **Nielsen gave an interview with Eastbay Catalog hyping the upcoming 'Kobe' shoe line.**

> *"The key to the design of 'The Kobe' was the collaboration process between the automotive and footwear industries, inspired by a unique design approach.*
>
> *Traditionally, footwear design starts with the inward and builds outward. With 'The Kobe2', we built the shoe from the outside in.*
>
> *The quality materials married with a unique design approach have led to one of the most innovative basketball shoes to hit the market in recent history."*

The reception of the 'most innovative basketball shoes' ranged from disbelief, rage, and outright confusion. Many critics called the model' blasphemy.' The new 'Kobe 2' line was universally panned by the public, with some even calling it 'The ugliest sports shoes in history.'

Once Kobe donned the sneakers, they looked even more hideous in person. Completely out of place on the basketball court, the basketball God looked like he was rocking a pair of toasters on his feet. (They even came with the appropriate toaster-like dull gray monochrome color.)

Needless to say, Kobe Bryant was disappointed and felt let down by Adidas.

From a PR standpoint and the impact on his image, Kobe didn't want to associate with a flawed product. Aside from its atrocious look, he believed the shoe didn't serve its purpose of helping an athlete. He was adamant about the impracticality of the shoe design, which led to frequent ankle injuries.

He believed the shoe must protect the player, and the protection must be the only 'North Star' in the creation and design of footwear.

Kobe Bryant was practical before anything else.

For him, shoes were much more than the sponsorship money and benefits. For Kobe Bryant, shoes were a weapon in the arsenal. He was looking for footwear that could give him even a slight competitive edge. At the very least, he wasn't expecting his sneakers to detract him from his game.

With Adidas shoes, Kobe had multiple ankle injuries due to impractical design.

The futuristic toaster-like 'Kobe 2' was Bryant's final shoe line for Adidas. It was clear to Kobe that the relationship was over, as the two sides had vastly different ideas for the future. In fact, as he later reflected, the clash of ideologies led to an unceremonious breakup. Adidas believed in style over substance, and they refused Kobe's creative input.

Not hesitating for a second, Bryant demanded to be released from the bond of the contract.

In an unprecedented manner for a sponsored athlete, he decided to buy out the remainder of his contract in 2002. Kobe would spend a 2002/2003 NBA season as the free agent in the world of sneakers before signing with NIKE in 2003. For the next 13 years, he remained exclusive with the American giant.

In those years, **Kobe and NIKE** produced some of the most iconic footwear in sports history. They shared a joint vision for the future of Kobe's sneakers: **Elegant in design, practical in its essence.**

The experience with Adidas taught Bryant a priceless lesson, for which he paid a whopping $8 million dollars.

Kobe learned he had to be personally involved from the start in any of the ventures he chose to pursue. Years later, his animosity towards Adidas was well-known and documented. As we got to find out, another lesson he learned and gracefully shared with the world was to *never deal with amateurs and never to accept incompetency.*

He believed people make a conscious choice to be professional, and that choice is a part of natural evolution and growth. Those who accepted mediocrity were those Kobe didn't want around him.

After splitting with the Germans, Kobe found a home with NIKE.

They had almost an ideal professional relationship, which only improved over the years. After his playing career, their partnership continued as Bryant assisted with the design process. NIKE believed in his creative input, and they appreciated his perspective.

They knew he was all about improvement, even in the tiniest of ways. In 2008, Kobe Bryant came to them with a strange request. He needed a few millimeters shaven off the bottom of his shoes to *get a 'hundredth of a second better reaction time.'*

Coincidentally or not, Kobe Bryant won the NBA MVP Award that year.

* * *

The Clash of Opposing Ideologies: The Rise & Fall of the Most Dynamic Duo in the History of Sports

Since emerging as a prodigy straight from high school, Kobe was labeled as the next great superstar of the NBA. In 1996, he joined the Los Angeles Lakers, and for the next 20 years, Kobe Bryant etched his name in basketball eternity. His legacy as a winner, a proven champion, and one of the greatest players of all time is undisputed.

Kobe wrote history in the iconic purple and gold jersey, but a chapter of that story includes another protagonist.

This man was the complete opposite of Kobe, the man who had vastly different life principles and the man with a seemingly larger-than-life persona and character.

In fact, on the very same day when Kobe Bryant signed for the Lakers, the GM of the team, Jerry West, caused a tectonic shift in the NBA by securing the services of the one and only **Shaquille O'Neal.**

Today, Shaq is known as the jolly big guy who works as a sports analyst for the TNT network, but back in his heyday, Shaq was a force of nature. Standing at 7ft1 and weighing over 350 pounds of solid muscle, O'Neal was the most dominant big man that ever played in the NBA. During the 90s and early 2000s, Shaquille was virtually unguardable.

In an era marked by the big man and in the league that featured superstars such as **Hakeem Olajuwon, David Robinson, Karl Malone, Charles Barkley, Patrick Ewing, Alonzo Morning**, and many others, *Shaq was unstoppable*.

Yet, as big and as powerful as he was, during those days in the 90s, Shaquille had a stigma attached to his name. He lacked the one thing that would immortalize his ultimate legacy. He couldn't lead his team to the NBA Championship, the pinnacle of any basketball career and a valid argument for defining individual basketball greatness.

From a pure character perspective standpoint, the story of Shaq and Kobe was almost writing itself.

The two men had polar opposite personalities and beliefs. Shaq was a loud, charismatic extrovert who thrived when at the center of attention. On the other hand, Kobe was somewhat of a loner, avoiding unnecessary distractions from the game of basketball.

Shaq loved to have fun and enjoy life to the fullest.
He was not a fan of practice or working hard throughout the season, as he relied on his talent and his physicality to get the job done.

Kobe Bryant was a ruthless professional.
Kobe's only love was basketball, and his sole mission in life was to be the greatest basketball player of all time. He spent every waking minute working hard to improve and get better. When he wasn't playing basketball, Kobe studied the game with the same level of intensity.

Shaq knew all too well about the infamous Mamba Mentality.
He had never played with a player who possessed the same will to compete and a desire to win.

Throughout his entire career, Shaq's modus operandi was rather simple. O'Neal was big, mean, and nasty. Due to his imposing size, O'Neal loved to play the role of a bully, which was his way of probing and testing the character of the other person. Naturally, people would usually back away from this mountain of a man when challenged and threatened.

Kobe Bryant, on the other hand, was no ordinary person. He had no intention of backing away from anyone. Throughout his career, and especially in his younger days, Kobe wasn't a stranger to physical altercations and fist fights on the court.

By the lockout-shortened season in 1999, the tension between the duo was brewing, just waiting to escalate further. The critical point occurred during practice when the two men engaged in a heated verbal exchange, quickly followed by a physical altercation.

In 2018, long after the incident took place, Shaquille and Kobe finally sat down and had a conversation where they reminisced about the good old days and shared less-known details about their stranded relationship.

> **Kobe**: *"I remember we were playing a pickup game. It was during a lockout season, and we played at South West College.*
>
> *We were on opposite teams and trash-talking. And you kept saying, 'Yeah, take that little b***h, take that little b***h.' I'm looking around, 'You talking to me?'*

> *"I said, 'Hold on, there ain't gonna be too many more of those.'*
>
> *And what did you say? 'What you gonna do about it?'.*
>
> *The next thing I knew, I saw a huge hand coming this way, and I remember going this way. And I remember throwing some lollipop s**t. As they pulled us apart, I remember you saying: "This madaf***er is crazy."*
>
> ***Shaq**: Hahaha, Yeah, yeah. I remember. I did say that. I thought you were crazy."*

No one had ever stood up to Shaq. Looking at the courageous youngster, Shaq was in disbelief. Since that particular day, however, O'Neal gained a newfound respect for Kobe Bryant. On the other hand, Kobe realized how much Shaq wanted to win the championship. The fact O'Neal couldn't win the title was eating away at him.

The fight was indeed a breaking point, but the event catalyzed the emergence of the Kobe-Shaq duo. They both realized they wanted to win, and the only way was together. However, the two 'Alpha-Males' with such dominant personalities needed a coach who would and who could manage them. By the start of the 1999/00 season, it was clear that **Del Harris** wasn't a man for that job.

The change was on the horizon, and soon, The LA Lakers put the entire NBA on notice.

GM Jerry West, a magician behind the scenes, convinced the legendary *Phil Jackson* to get back into the game. After Chicago, he wowed never to coach again, but the challenge of establishing his status as the greatest NBA coach of all time was too alluring to refuse.

Under the guidance of Phil Jackson, the Los Angeles Lakers dynasty was born. **Kobe-Shaq duo terrorized the league**, with the Lakers breaking numerous records throughout the season and playoff. The Lakers seemed invincible with both superstars in their prime, with a decent supporting cast, and with a proven winner behind the helm.

Success was inevitable.

But just like with any great empire in the history of civilization, the collapse started from within. As soon as our duo won the title, the apparent differences between Bryant and O'Neal emerged to the surface.

Shaquille O'Neal won his first NBA title. In the process, the big man dominated the league, winning the MVP award. In Shaq's mind, he was the best player in the league, with nothing else to prove to anybody. He could enjoy and have some fun in the summer and the off-season. Shaq knew he could rely on his co-star, the generational talent, to do the hard work.

Kobe Bryant achieved his boyhood dream of winning the championship in the Lakers jersey. In only his fourth season, Kobe became the best two-way player in the league. In addition to his stellar offense, which produced 23 points with high efficiency, Kobe showcased a world-class defense.

He worked tirelessly during the previous summer, and as always, the hard work paid off. The NBA recognized Bryant for his defensive efforts with a first-team selection, a reward that Kobe was especially proud of. After winning the title, Kobe realized how much work had yet to be done. He still had weakness in his armor, and the upcoming off-season was the ideal time to improve his game.

Kobe wasn't planning on settling with just one championship and a few awards. His goals extended way beyond being the best in the NBA today. He wanted to be the greatest player ever.

On his road to greatness, Kobe was striving for perfection. He knew perfection was an unattainable ideal, but he did everything he could to get as close as possible. Anything less than his best would mean Kobe wasn't *outworking his potential*, which was a personal philosophy he picked up early in life.

> *"He didn't take a single breath from the championships to October, the beginning of the season. He wanted to annihilate everyone. He wasn't gonna settle until he was recognized as the best player in the league."*
>
> *— Phil Jackson speaking about Kobe's professionalism and ideology during their 2000–2002 historic run*

Despite winning two more championships, the Shaq-Kobe duo was already on borrowed time. With each passing year, the rift between the two stars was getting wider. With each subsequent season, the intensity of the rivalry and power struggle gradually increased. Both of them believed to be the rightful leader of the team. Both believed the root cause of the issue lay in the other one.

Throughout the years, Shaq was more vocal, especially when speaking to the press. On more than one occasion, Shaq called out Kobe for his individualism, critiquing him for not being a team player. He knew how to play the media, and they always danced to his tune.

Since the emergence of the duo, Shaq has forced the "Big Brother -Little Brother" narrative. While he was older than Bryant, in many ways, Kobe was always the more mature brother.

Throughout his entire career, Shaquille O'Neal never hesitated to speak up and make noise, even to the detriment of the team. Self-proclaimed 'Chief Marketer' had magnetic charisma and knew how to keep the spotlight on himself. Kobe was annoyed with Shaq's media handling, as he would inevitably be entangled in any drama surrounding the big man.

Kobe's problem with Shaquille was much deeper than surface-level noise.

Throughout the years, Shaq often talked about being the team leader yet rarely conducted as one. O'Neal's poor work ethic affected the entire team and their chances of winning. Although he would make a full recovery and be in peek form right around the playoff, O'Neal's lack of fitness and non-existent professionalism were a growing concern.

While Shaq was out, it was Kobe who carried the Lakers, displaying an otherworldly level of basketball prowess. Bryant, who was head and shoulder above the rest of the league, would take the back seat once the big man returned from absence.

Kobe was willing to subordinate his ego despite believing Shaq didn't deserve to lead the team. Yet, Kobe played whatever coach Phil wanted him to play because he was a model professional at his core. He was willing to play whichever role was needed as long as they were winning.

In 2004, after the Lakers failed against the Pistons in the playoff final, Kobe found himself at the crossroads of life.

Bryant's contract was expiring in the summer, and after seven years in the Los Angeles Lakers, he pondered his future. He was at the point in his career where his all-time status was at stake.

Despite winning three championship rings and countless individual awards, Kobe Bryant was disputed. Often seen as Shaq's sidekick, Bryant was accustomed to unfair public treatment. He never bothered with the opinion of those who never played professionally in the league. Bryant treated the media as he viewed them - like a necessary part of the NBA machinery.

However, once Shaq started talking publicly and doubting Kobe's chances of winning without him, Bryant took his words as a personal challenge.

O'Neal's repeated jabs and statements gave Kobe a newfound

purpose. As unfair as it is, he knew his legacy would one day be judged in conjunction with O'Neal's. He realized that in order to secure his place as one of the greatest, he would have to go his separate ways from Shaq.

Simply, Kobe wanted to prove he could win without Shaquille O'Neal.

The hardest part was parting ways with his beloved Lakers. He felt honor and pride every time he wore the Lakers uniform. In LA, he felt at home. Bryant even contemplated staying in LA with the status quo intact. He could play second fiddle to O'Neal; hypothetically, they could've won another two or three titles.

If he opted to stay with O'Neal, Kobe knew what that option meant. He would have to sacrifice his personal game, just like he'd been doing for the last few years. Even if he accepted the same faith as every previous year, Kobe didn't believe the Lakers could win anymore. He didn't believe that playing and sacrificing for Shaq would bring them any championships again.

As difficult as it was, Kobe couldn't compromise his integrity, especially in the wake of Shaq's public comments and statements. Bryant was ready to leave the Los Angeles Lakers.

Fortunately, he didn't have to.

The Los Angeles Lakers wanted to keep Kobe at all costs, even if it meant trading Shaquille O'Neal. Behind the scenes, Shaq became increasingly more difficult to handle. Despite being the highest-paid player in the squad by a far margin, Shaq wanted a new contract and more money for his services. In addition, O'Neal was 32 years old, with a history of injuries and a chronic lack of fitness.

Despite having three more years on his lucrative contract, the Lakers traded Shaquille O'Neal to Miami on July 14, 2004, effectively ending a Los Angeles Lakers dynasty. The very next day, Kobe Bryant signed a new 7-year deal worth $136 million dollars. With these two moves, the Lakers welcomed a new era of basketball.

The Aftermath of the Crumble

The most dynamic duo in the history of sports won three consecutive championships. Throughout the span of eight years they played together, the tandem terrorized the league, breaking numerous records in the process. The duo of Kobe and Shaq gave the fans countless treasured memories throughout their memorable run.

Due to their polar opposite life philosophies and vastly different personalities, Kobe and Shaq were destined to eventually go their separate ways. After O'Neal left, the two had a strained relationship for many years. Shaq would occasionally fire a poisonous arrow toward his former co-star, stirring up controversy once again. He loved all the attention he could get, and talking about Kobe would ensure his place in the media spotlight. As usual, Kobe used all the negativity and criticism to fuel his journey to greatness.

Interestingly, Bryant remained adamant about his stance on his former teammate and leader. He believed Shaq could've been the greatest player in the history of the game if he wanted to. In turn, the team could've won more titles, and both men would cement their respective legacies as all-time greats.

After the split, Bryant refused to play the media game and speak negatively about his former partner, other than wishing him the best in future endeavors. Despite not talking publicly about their relationship, Kobe remained firm in his opinion that O'Neal's lack of work ethic and professionalism was one of the reasons they had to go their separate ways.

The reason for the split, explained years later by the big man himself, was Shaq's desire to get a better contract and more money. Unlike Kobe, he wasn't a Laker growing up, and his dreams had nothing to do with purple and gold. Like Bryant, O'Neal was also a man of principles and made a decision according to his ideology and life perspective.

There was certainly no love lost between the two, but in 2009, the beef they had throughout the years had been squashed once and for all.

The All-Star game in Phoenix brought the two men together for the one last time as they represented the Western Conference in an annual clash against their Eastern counterparts. At this stage of their careers, Shaq and Kobe were on different points of their respective journeys. At age 37, O'Neal's career slowly unwinded, and retirement seemed closer than ever. Bryant was still in pursuit of another championship(s), which he finally won that year. Kobe would repeat the accomplishment the following year after leading his Lakers against their Arch-Enemy, the Boston Celtics, in 2010.

For that one night in Phoenix, though, the future didn't matter. It was all about reliving the past moments of glory.

O'Neal and Bryant led the Western Conference team in a 146–119 win against the East. Once revered tandem turned back the clock in a vintage *Kobe-Shaq performance.*

Fittingly, the duo won the NBA All-Star co-MVP award.

As usual, the story of the former co-stars was the headline of the All-Star. The entire world tuned in to witness the historical moment of reunion. Throughout the weekend, O'Neal and Bryant took a stroll down memory lane, reminiscing about the good old days.

Once fierce rivals, both men have matured to a point where they could objectively look back at their era of dominance and marvel at their joint accomplishments. Shaq and Kobe certainly appreciated what they had. They were grateful for the moments and appreciative of each other. Ultimately, both of them realized that throughout all the friction, they pushed each other to absolute limits. They made each other evolve into a better version of themselves.

After the game, in a move that forever put their past behind them, **Kobe Bryant relinquished the trophy in favor of Shaquille O'Neal.** He knew the physical award and memento

UNCOMPROMISING INTEGRITY

would mean the world to Shaq's 9-year-old son. **Shareef O'Neal** was mesmerized by Kobe Bryant, who was his basketball idol. Throughout the weekend in Phoenix, the three of them spent a lot of time together, and Kobe was inspired by young Shareef and his love for the game of basketball.

After all, trophies come and go. Kobe knew that. He had more trophies and awards than he could fit in a storage room.

> *In Kobe's mind, what was one more trophy compared to the excitement and happiness of a child who idolizes you?*

Driven by that particular belief and life perspective, he gave Shaq the trophy and asked him to give it to his friend Shareef. With this heartfelt move and newfound admiration for each other, Kobe and Shaq moved on to new chapters of their lives.

Once he handed the trophy to O'Neal, he jokingly added his closet was full of individual trophies. The space was running out, and he still needed one more to complete the collection. Kobe alluded to the most prestigious individual award in the NBA.

The trophy that eluded Kobe was awarded to the best player of the final series in the playoffs - **The Finals MVP.** *The trophy* **symbolizes the winner who led his team to glory.** The award for best player in the most important game series epitomizes individual greatness.

Sure enough, 'The Mamba' delivered his promise to Shaq that

101

weekend in Phoenix, as he won two more NBA Championships and two more Finals MVP awards in 2009 and 2010, respectively.

6

Relentless Desire & Mental Warfare

> *"People look at my competitive spirit, and they automatically attach it to the thing that's most similar, most easily recognizable, which is Michael [Jordan's] competitive spirit.*
>
> *I'm different.*
>
> *I enjoy building. I enjoy the process of putting the puzzle together, and then the byproduct of that, the consequence of that, is beating somebody. That becomes the cherry on top, the icing on the cake."*

Over the years, The Mamba Mentality became somewhat synonymous with Bryant's ferocious intensity, his drive to compete, and his unwavering desire to win. Kobe's relentless will to win at any cost has been immortalized in numerous stories of his contemporaries. All of them seem to support the notion of Kobe as a relentless competitor with an incredible mind and basketball intelligence.

Kobe was a master at breaking people's spirits. Always on the lookout for a way to win, exposing any weakness to Bryant could have detrimental consequences. He loved to break his 'enemy's' will, and he thrived in their struggle to stop him. He enjoyed seeing the defeated looks in their eyes. From the perspective of his peers in the NBA, playing against Kobe required maximum effort and maximum focus. Both of these are extremely difficult to sustain for the duration of the entire game.

As a competitor and opponent, he seemed to be different than any other.

Kobe's understanding of human psychology, combined with his intelligence and ruthless approach to the game of basketball, made him a genuinely feared and dreaded opponent for any player on any given night.

There seems to be a common thread between Bryant's desire to win and his ability to do anything necessary to achieve victory.

By all accounts, Kobe's desire to win was a force to be reckoned with. The competitive drive, one of The Mamba Mentality trademark qualities, was something Kobe couldn't really control. The urge to play basketball, dominate the opponent, and win the game was the driving force in his life.

Bryant's willingness to go to extremes made him the fiercest competitor we all remember him as. Even as a young player looking at his craft, *Kobe realized how much was within his control. He made a conscious decision to learn the nuances of the game, and he studied the subject of basketball with lifelong devotion and passion.*

Unlike the need to win, which seemed inherent in his DNA, Kobe's basketball intelligence and his success on the court grew increasingly larger once he approached the game as if it were a battleground. As a child, he gravitated toward the subject of history. As a teenager, he read biographies of famous leaders, generals, and other prominent historical figures.

In fact, his philosophy on basketball drew direct inspiration from the ancient *Chinese military text,* ***The Art of War.***

Written by the famous Chinese general and strategist ***Sun Tzu***, the ancient military document is comprised of 13 chapters that are devoted to the strategic and tactical aspects of warfare. **The Art of War explains in detail how to behave in battle and, more importantly, how to win.**

Aside from specific tips on combat and strategy, this ancient military document has a profound philosophical side to it. In his writings, Sun Tzu argues the use of intelligence over brute force and teaches how to win the war the smart way. Sun Tzu is considered one of history's finest military tacticians and analysts. His teachings and strategies formed the basis of advanced military training for millennia to come.

The beauty of The Art of War is that its wisdom can be applied to

modern life in times of peace. The book emphasizes preparation above anything else, which is something Kobe took to heart.

Kobe was a student of the game, and he knew the ins and outs of each team and each individual player in the league. Before anything else, he relied on preparation and planning. By the time he stepped on the court to play the game, Kobe Bryant already knew how systematically to destroy the opponent.

Years later, and in many interviews, Kobe talked in length about the psychological aspect of basketball, specifically the role of mental warfare.

> *"There would be certain teams that had a player that they just signed to a max contract. And then a supporting player who was up for the free agency, which they hadn't signed yet.*
>
> *So when we played them during the season, I'm saying, ok, here's what we're going to do:*
>
> *We're going to double-team the guy that hasn't gotten a max contract yet. We're not gonna let him get a shot off. And then we're going to single-cover the guy that has the max contract, and then watch the guy that doesn't have the max contract bitch and complain about not getting the ball all night long, and watch them divide each other.*
>
> *Those are the little, subtle things we would do, and they come from observation and understanding your opponent."*

It was no secret — In order to win, Kobe Bryant looked for any way possible to gain a competitive advantage over his opponents. Since he was a child, before stepping on the court, he would ask himself: *'How can I win against this particular opponent?'*

As a six-year-old playing against other six-year-olds in Italy, Kobe realized none of the other kids knew how to use their left hand. He would then make them dribble to their left, quickly steal the ball, and score an easy layup. Bryant jokingly reminisced on the earliest days in Italy, saying he would score 50 points by doing this one simple thing: *playing to the opponent's weakness.*

On the constant quest to find different ways to win, while he was still a kid, Kobe discovered a new way of breaking the opponent and simultaneously increasing his chances of winning. He noticed how other kids were often emotionally unstable, and any little outside interference could throw them off their usual game.

Barely a teenager, Kobe Bryant relied on psychological warfare with one goal in mind:
To find and exploit a weakness in the opponent's armor. Once you do, break their will and destroy them in a game.

Other kids, much like other grown men years later, were often wary and uneasy around Kobe. He was unpredictable in demeanor and aloof in personality. He was charming and sophisticated, yet he kept his distance.

Bryant was often unpleasant and radical with his methods, playing every single possession as if it was his last and bringing intensity the opposition had never experienced before.

The message he sent to his opponents was always loud and clear: *I want to destroy and humiliate you, and I will find a way to win.*

Kobe was vicious in his desire to be the greatest ever. Alongside his other qualities, such as impeccable work ethic, professionalism, confidence, and mental resilience, Kobe Bryant firmly established himself as one of basketball's greatest players.

On the court, he had a superior intellect and an unparalleled ability to outsmart the opponent in any situation. He was skilled enough to do whatever he wanted to the opposition and was certainly willing to do whatever was necessary to win. On top of that, no player in the game's history devoted himself to basketball as much as Kobe Bryant did. He lived for basketball, and he spent every waking moment thinking about different ways he could get better.

After the 2003/2004 season in particular, when he played the entire year fighting for his freedom while leading the Lakers to the NBA Finals, Kobe's mental toughness was unquestioned. The man seemingly shut off any emotions and played the game with laser-like focus. Bryant played with the highest intensity while making rational and often split-second decisions that made all the difference. Once he was in the zone, the man was unstoppable.

Kobe's relentless ferocity, desire to win, and cerebral ap-

proach to the game of basketball, mentioned in many tales of his contemporaries, came from the most unexpected circumstances. This brilliant form of **psychological offense emerged as a defense mechanism at first.**

As a junior in the summer league, Kobe had to make a stand against other boys who believed he was weak. The other kids tried to intimidate and bully Kobe. Coming from Italy, he was always the outsider among his peers. Some of them made a mistake thinking they could mentally break down this 'kid from Italy,' a kid many perceived as the biggest threat on the basketball court.

Kobe Bryant wasn't planning on backing down from the attackers. On the contrary, he devised a strategy for mentally breaking down his opponents.

He didn't have to say a word to these kids. He let his attitude and behavior do all the talking. He was the hardest-working player in the summer league camp, and no one was even close in terms of commitment to the game. Getting up every morning at 4 AM and being in the gym by 5 AM, Kobe Bryant set the standard of excellence from day one.

Other kids, especially his rivals, would see him work out and practice. Sweat dripping off him, Kobe intensely works out on his jump shot or another element of his game. On other occasions, as soon as he finished his lunch at the cafeteria, he would head to the gym to practice. He would practice without the ball for the next hour and a half, doing the most common basketball drills in the playbook.

All the young players in the summer league camp soon realized a frightening truth. Kobe doesn't stop. This kid spends all of his time working out in the gym, and with each passing day, he is getting better and better.

The scene would put them in a bit of a conundrum. If they don't do anything, they will inevitably fall behind, and they know it. On the other hand, if they follow this kid and join, it would make them look weak.

In any case, Kobe couldn't care less about what they'd decided. He knew he had won already. He was inside their minds and had a mental edge over them.

During the first days of the summer camp, Kobe had already analyzed each and every one of the other players. He knew about their weakness and how to exploit them, just as he was aware of their strengths. Once on the court, he wanted to annihilate and humiliate everybody else, and his game reflected his mindset. By his own admission, his only job on the court was to destroy the opponent and, of course, win the game.

Little did anyone know, but even back then, during the summer league, Kobe Bryant was on a mission. He felt a sense of purpose in his craft and would devote himself to the game of basketball.

"At the age of 13,14, I would size you up from head to toe.

How do you approach the game? Are you silly and goofy about it? Do you rely purely on athletic abilities and God-given talent, or is there a thought and a skill in your game?

I would look at you and see what you do.

Is your game improving and evolving? Are you still doing the same things at 17 that you were doing when you were 15?

If you are, and your game is still the same, you are in big trouble.
And I will let you know about it." – Kobe Bryant on screening the competition.

At age 13, Kobe Bryant had a 'Kill List.'

The list consisted of high school players in the entire country, ranked by the prestigious '*Street and Smith* basketball magazine.

During his time at Lower Marion High School, the 'experts' from the magazine ranked Kobe at #57. In their defense, Kobe Bryant was unknown at the time. As a teenager, his physicality left much to be desired. He was a scrawny kid, at 6ft4 and 160 pounds soaking wet; some even went as far as calling him soft and weak.

He took the criticism and the rankings as fuel, working harder than ever before.

Kobe's mission in high school was to hunt down all the players that were ranked above him. He would study each and every one of them, the teams they played for, their strengths and weaknesses, and he would go to work.

Bryant would soon check off each player placed above him on that arbitrary rankings.

One by one, until he crossed the first name on that list, Kobe didn't stop in his pursuit. Yet, his eyes were set on a much larger prize.

* * *

On the high school basketball circuit, Kobe Bryant was a sensation.

Every major college in the US wanted him in their ranks. In the eyes of the legendary college basketball coach, *Mike Krzyzewski*, the man who witnessed the ascension of many basketball greats, **Kobe Bryant was the best high school player in history.**

For Krzyzewski, **Kobe was the best because he was different from the rest.**

"From all the high school players I've seen, I thought Kobe, as the high school player, was the best.

He wasn't a kid playing back then. He played the game intelligently. He carried himself in a way that was way beyond his years.

He obviously had this incredible ability to score, and when he was on the court, he hurt the other team with his mere presence. The only other player I can compare him to is Michael Jordan during his time at North Carolina. He had the same effect on the court."

— Mike Krzyzewski, the head coach of Duke University (1980–2022)

* * *

Passing of The Torch

After conquering high school basketball and skipping college altogether, Kobe's dreams started unfolding in front of his eyes. Everything he worked so hard for is finally coming to fruition. As a kid, he visualized the famous NBA Draft Lottery night, and now he has arrived. The next morning, he was in the gym at 4 AM, working and preparing for the first season in his career.

Bryant came into the NBA league with the same approach and desire to dominate, win, and be the best. Although still just a teenager, **The Mamba Mentality was taking shape on the worldwide stage.**

Similarly, he came into the NBA with the chip on his shoulder, the one he so heavily relied on throughout his entire career. As the youngest player in the league and as a boy amongst men, Kobe felt like an outsider. Once again, he gladly accepted the role he portrayed his entire life. The role only served as fuel on his journey to basketball greatness.

Bryant wanted to prove himself from day one. He would go hard at his teammates in LA during practice. Fearless on both ends of the court, he had the same intensity in his game, combined with an equal desire to win, as **arguably the greatest player ever — Michael Jordan.** MJ is the epitome of the ultimate winner and champion. In fact, to any basketball player coming into the NBA league, Jordan was the benchmark for greatness.

By the same token, Michael's relentlessness on the court became a measuring stick for Kobe. He wanted to be the greatest player of all time, and Kobe knew that the only way to do it was to match and exceed Jordan's relentless ferocity, which was the quality Kobe believed led Michael to win six NBA Championships.

In fact, Kobe Bryant was the only one who could match Jordan's desire to win, and he, much like Michael, had the ability and willingness to go to any lengths for a victory.

Bryant never hid the fact he based his playing style on Jordan's, and his basketball move-set was eerily similar to Michael's. Just like he 'stole' certain moves from **Magic Johnson, James Worthy, Byron Scott**, and many others, Kobe saw something else he could 'steal' from Jordan's bag of tricks.

What Bryant particularly admired and modeled was Michael's aura of invincibility. Jordan had a menacing presence. The level of fear he inspired in others was both insane and ridiculous. MJ would often beat the opponent before the game even started.

Michael would mentally break down his direct guard in the tunnel, either by verbally challenging him or, conversely, not saying a single word the entire game. He tailored his approach and strategy based on the specific opponent for that game. After all, just like Kobe, Jordan knew each and every player from each and every team. Preparation was a critical weapon in Michael's arsenal.

On the court, MJ was capable of almost anything. His mastery of the game was unparalleled. Jordan often went to extreme lengths for victory, and he was willing to break the enemy's morale by any means necessary. Michael enjoyed humiliating anyone who tried to guard him.

Michael was also an unusually intelligent and perceptive individual. He, much like Kobe, understood the nature of the human character. He gladly used any weakness of the opponent as leverage on the way to victory.

MJ was looking for any way to win, even if it meant waging a psychological war on the battlefield of the mind. Among his peers in the NBA, as much as he was revered for all his achievements, *Jordan was dreaded for his demeanor, personality, and unwavering desire to compete and win.*

While he was still in high school, Kobe used to work with the Philadelphia 76ers, and he was eager to know what it was like playing against Michael Jordan. Much to his surprise, Jordan's peers and adversaries on the court described MJ as 'The Black Jesus' and 'Air Jordan.'

Reggie Miller, NBA Hall of Famer and 5x NBA All-Star, pleaded to Kobe not to challenge the great MJ, whom he referred to as 'The Black Cat.' Baffled by the response but without missing a beat, Bryant famously said: *"Ok. You can call me the Caramel Cat* *from now on."*

Challenging the Greatest of All Time is exactly what Kobe Bryant did the first time they squared off.

When he first entered a league as a teenager, MJ got the best of Kobe almost every time they played. While both of them had almost equal skills, Michael was better because he had experience on his side, an invaluable resource available a bit later in life.

Despite the usual outcome, Kobe wasn't going to be discouraged. Never losing a step, he was right there on the next play. In fact, during the games, he gravitated toward Michael. Cameras would often catch the two men chatting and laughing.

Kobe thrived in the challenge of beating the greatest.
In 1998, During his sophomore year in the league, in the middle of the All-Star game, Kobe challenged MJ to a 1–1 duel. Michael was both amused and flattered by the playfully admiring teenager determined to come after him. They spent much time during the All-Star Weekend, and MJ, usually reserved, graciously shared knowledge with the young student. Michael recognized many of his character traits in this 18-year-old.

Bryant had the same desire to win, the desire that fueled MJ when he first came into the league in 1984. It was clear as a day: Kobe Bryant and Michael Jordan were cut from the same cloth.

Kobe was like a sponge, taking all the knowledge and wisdom

from the Greatest of All Time.

> *"I was getting schooled for a baseline dunk the first time I matched up with him. It was the coolest thing. I've seen that spin a million times. I knew what he was gonna do, and I couldn't stop him. How cool is that?"*
>
> *— Kobe on his first-ever matchup against Michael Jordan*

From his earliest days in the league, MJ took Kobe under his wing. He assumed the role of a mentor to Bryant, who was ready to be the student. Jordan described their relationship as a **'nuisance that turned into love over a relatively short period of time.'**

Part of Jordan's mystique was simply in his reserved demeanor, similar to his much younger counterpart. Unlike other superstars in the league, striving for attention, MJ wasn't available or just as easily reachable. The man preferred his own company. Understandably, as one of the rare global superstars who transcended the game, Jordan had to be careful about his associations, and he had to be selective about the people he allowed in his life.

As much as Michael tried to ignore the youngster, Kobe wasn't giving up. He wanted to make the connection and learn from the greatest, and eventually, their relationship turned from 'a nuisance' into love and mutual respect. (The dynamic of their relationship has been beautifully illustrated in *'The Last Dance,'* the 10-part Netflix docuseries that followed Michael Jordan and the Chicago Bulls during the 1998 NBA season.)

In many ways, Kobe and Michael were a mirror image of one another. Over time, their acquaintance blossomed into a genuine friendship and eventually into a bond as strong as the brotherhood. While Michael was enjoying his second retirement, Kobe had already proved himself. He established a reputation as an elite guard, and more importantly, he won championships.

In 2001, Michael Jordan came out of retirement and briefly played for the *Washington Wizards.* The two men would square up a handful of times during the following couple of seasons, and both were particularly inspired when playing against the other.

The location of their final battle was the Staples Center.

Michael Jordan's retirement tour took the Washington Wizards to Los Angeles. Naturally, the center stage was reserved for the de facto *'**Passing of the torch'*** moment the entire world was waiting to see. The exclusive media narrative leading up to the game was about the direct duel between Kobe and MJ.

The last time they played against each other, under the brightest lights of Los Angeles, the Greatest Player of All-Time, was in serious trouble. Michael had no idea what was coming. Two weeks before, Jordan made a critical mistake without even realizing it.

118

In their previous game in Washington, as a sign of respect, Kobe Bryant wore a 'Jordan' model of Nike shoes. Through the symbolic gesture, Kobe wanted to pay respect to his mentor and friend, the greatest master of the game. The match was a tight contest, but eventually, the *Wizards* prevailed and won the game.

Afterward, the two teams traded handshakes and hugs. As Michael walked away, he turned and said to Bryant:

> '' You know, you can wear those shoes, but you ain't never gonna fill them."
> — Jordan's passing comment to Kobe Bryant.

Jordan's co-star at the time, the former Washington Wizards All-Star **Gilbert Arenas,** confirmed the story that was considered just a rumor for over a decade.

Apparently, Kobe was angry and hurt by the seemingly innocent remark, and he hadn't spoken to his team in two weeks while mentally and tactically preparing for the final duel.

Once his teammates heard the reason for Kobe's strange behavior, they knew exactly how the match would play out. Kobe visualized and rehearsed the reception for his friend, and he wanted to make sure Jordan enjoyed the performance.

As a sign of the utmost respect toward the master of the game, Kobe couldn't give him anything less than what he was capable of. He saved something special as a parting gift to his mentor, a historic spectacle to remember in retirement.

Kobe Bryant scored 55 points on Michael Jordan and the rest of his supporting cast. More impressively, Bryant scored 42 points in the first half of the game, playing less than 20 minutes. Kobe played with a vengeance, yet his demeanor was calm, calculated, and, eventually, playful.

From the opening minute, Kobe was locked in the game and intense as if he was playing game seven of the NBA Finals. He was in the zone, running across the floor and crushing Washington on both ends of the floor. There were other players on the court, but in this particular game, they were just idle spectators.

The duel was between The Greatest of All Time and The Greatest of Today.

Jordan certainly held his own against a ferocious competitor and inspired opponent. Yet on this night, even the great Michael Jordan couldn't compete with Kobe Bryant. Halfway through the second quarter, after another spectacular dunk from Kobe, the cameras zoomed in on MJ, who was sitting on the bench.

With a towel hanging across his head, trying to catch his breath, it finally dawned on Michael.

Jordan realized what was happening in front of his eyes, and he knew exactly what he did to deserve this parting gift. Michael was seen smiling and nodding in agreement, knowing he would've done the same thing.

After the game ended in a blowout Lakers win, the two masters hugged and embraced. In their final duel, Kobe sent his friend off to retirement with a parting gift, reminding Michael the game of basketball was in good hands.

As MJ enjoyed his final retirement, the game kept evolving, and basketball entered a new era. Just like the previous decade belonged to Jordan, the era of 2000s basketball was undoubtedly the Era of Kobe Bryant.

7

Evolution & Leadership

> *"Being a leader, it's the art of trying to find the balance, the right times with each individual and what they need at that moment. It requires looking outward as opposed to looking inside.*
>
> *Everybody has a different journey. There is power in understanding the journey of others to help create your own."*

In 2004, The Los Angeles Lakers found themselves in uncharted territory.

The board and management had to decide on the franchise's long-term future. The rising tension between the two major fractions in the locker room finally escalated. On the one side, the big man Shaquille O'Neal, standing on the other, was Kobe Bryant. The locker room was divided between those who supported Shaq and those players who believed Kobe was the rightful leader of the team.

The season ended in catastrophe, losing in the Finals against the Detroit Pistons. Shaquille wanted more money, Kobe wanted to leave, and Jackson refused to come back the next year if Bryant was still on the team.

The executive board decided to trade Shaq, allow Phil's contract to expire, and sign a new 7-year deal with Bryant. With this gesture, he was given the franchise keys and expected to lead the Lakers to future glory. The media and the public met the decision with heavy skepticism.

Kobe's reputation took a massive blow in the last year, partly due to his case trial in Colorado and partly due to his highly publicized feud with Shaq.

At the time, the consensus belief was that Kobe was the one responsible for the destruction of the Lakers dynasty. Until years later, when it was discovered O'Neal's demands were ridiculous, Kobe was the villain in that particular story.

Bryant couldn't care less about the opinions of others. He used the negativity as fuel for his late nights and early-morning workouts, just like he had done so many times before. His biggest challenge was in front of him, and Kobe had to learn how to win without Shaquille. He had to learn how to lead his team to victory.

Despite playing the game of his life, Kobe was surrounded by a sub-par supporting cast for the next few years. The team's morale was in free fall, and Kobe couldn't find a common language with those he was meant to lead.

Individually, Bryant stepped up to the challenge, leading the league in various categories.
Kobe was the league's second-leading scorer at 27.6 points per game, but ultimately his heroics failed. Undoubtedly, he was the best player in the league, but the team was abysmal. The Lakers went 34−48, missing the playoffs for the first time in over a decade.

The year signified a drop in Bryant's overall status in the NBA, as he did not make the NBA All-Defensive Team and was also demoted to the All-NBA Third Team. To make things worse for Kobe and the Lakers, Shaq won the title in his first year with his new team, Miami Heat. The future looked grim to any Laker fan during that year.

However, luck would smile on the Lakers in 2005. Phil Jackson, the greatest coach of all time, abruptly ended his retirement and returned to the 'City of Angels.'

While he was away, Phil Jackson published a book titled "*The Last Season: A Team in Search of Its Soul*," where he publicly disposed of the dirty laundry from the infamous 2004 Lakers season. In it, among many other juicy details, Phil called Bryant uncoachable and difficult to work with.

> *"Life is too short to hold grudges. We are here to win."*
> *— Kobe's exclusive statement once Phil Jackson returned*

as head coach.

Indeed, *'The Zen Master'* was pleasantly surprised by this version of his student. Kobe, who welcomed him back, seemed more mature and wise.

Understandably, given all the circumstances during 2004 that 'forced' Bryant to grow. In a relatively short span of time, he went from being on top of the world to fighting for freedom. To make things worse, his team was falling apart, and he was accused of the Lakers' destruction.

During that particular time, Kobe did a lot of soul-searching and reflection. The entire ordeal with the trial was a paradigm shift for Kobe. He started looking at life with different sets of eyes.

Kobe Bryant came out of the storm as a wiser and better version of himself.

Yet, one thing remained a constant. Kobe wanted to win championships, and now more than ever. With Jackson returning, the offense revolved around Bryant. The triangle offense Kobe knew so well, the method that brought them three championships, was a proven recipe for success.

With Jackson's influence, Kobe's maturation and evolution were inevitable. This time around, the two men had much better communication. As a result, Kobe's relationship with his teammates improved. The Lakers were finally looking like a team.

Yet, on the court, where it matters the most, the Lakers couldn't win.

For the next few seasons, Kobe Bryant led almost every individual statistical category in the NBA league. Despite Kobe's brilliance, he couldn't lead his team to the ultimate prize, the NBA championship.

In the season 2005/2006, Kobe Bryant was unstoppable, posting some of the most impressive statistical numbers in the league's history. He led the league in points per game with 35,4, and he won his first scoring title. In addition, Kobe set Lakers single-season franchise records for most 40-point games (27) and most points scored (2,832). In January, when the playoff spot was on the line, and the team struggled to make the postseason, Kobe Bryant stepped up and averaged 43,4 points per game.

2006/2007 was more of the same for the Lakers, with Kobe individually dominating the league in every conceivable fashion. Yet, the team couldn't overcome the first hurdle, the first round of the NBA playoffs. Just like the year before, the Lakers ran into the *Phoenix Suns* in the first round of the playoffs. Just like the year before, the *Suns* beat them again, ending yet another disappointing Lakers season.

After two years of growth and learning from experience, 2008 seemed like the year of Purple and Gold.

Although it took a while for all the right pieces to fall into place, with the arrival of **Pau Gasol** in February, the Lakers were ready for a shot at the title. Kobe Bryant had another outstanding season. He rightfully won an *MVP award* and was selected to an *NBA All-Defensive First Team.* In fact, by the end of the regular season and the beginning of the 2008 playoffs, the Lakers looked unstoppable after clinching the number one spot in the Western Conference.

The only team that could stop them from winning the title was their **arch-rival, Boston Celtics**. Over at the eastern conference, Boston was running through the opposition with ease, with their "Big 3" consisting of **Paul Pierce, Ray Allen, and Kevin Garnet.** In addition to all of these superstars, the Celtics had incredible role players on the bench who could step in and contribute when needed.

What many predicted at the start of the season eventually came to fruition in the NBA finals. The Clash of the Titans for the most coveted prize — The NBA Championship. After four long and painful years since the defeat against the Detroit Pistons, the Lakers were back in the NBA Finals.

With pride and legacy on the line, Boston Celtics vs. Los Angeles Lakers is one of the most intense rivalries in sports history. And, now, it was time for Kobe Bryant to lead the Lakers to glory and etch his name into the basketball eternity.

Unfortunately, some things in life are just not meant to be.

In a grueling physical series, Boston found and implemented a winning strategy, which was primarily to contain Bryant on the defensive end of the floor. The rest of the Lakers team was completely shut from Kobe, failing to make any significant contribution to the series. The Celtics won the series 4−2, as Bryant, the reigning MVP, failed to lead his team to the championship.

Bryant underperformed on the grandest stage and under the brightest lights.

Yet, Kobe's greatest defeat made him learn a priceless lesson about compassion, empathy, and leadership.

* * *

It's Always Darkest Before the Dawn: Personal Evolution & Compassionate Leadership

Growing up, Kobe was a Lakers fan full and through. Considering how much he knew about the Lakers organization, the players, and moments in LA's glorious history, Bryant could easily be classified as a die-hard fan, which is a notion he gladly embraced. Since he was a toddler wearing a fitting little purple jersey, Kobe daydreamed and visualized the day he'd lift the NBA championship high above his head.

One of his biggest dreams was to be involved in the historic rivalry with the Celtics, just like ***Magic***, ***Worthy***, and ***Kareem*** were all those years ago. More importantly, he wanted to beat the Boston Celtics for the championship. In his mind, coming out on top and winning against such a bitter rival would define his legacy as much as his individual success.

After the loss in Boston, the team came back to Los Angeles.

Kobe locked himself in the room, and he spent the entire night reflecting on the game, analyzing the entire season, and pondering his future. For the first time in his career, a sudden feeling of unease crept in on him. As unfair as it might be, he knew his basketball legacy would be judged based on the success and championships he won without Shaquille O'Neal.

That night, for the first time, Kobe thought how difficult it might be for him and his team to get another chance at the championship. For the first time in a very long time, Self-Doubt emerged in the back of his mind.

He recollected the events years after, thinking to himself:
"Maybe this was it. Maybe it's not in the cards for me to win another one."

Kobe allowed himself to feel self-doubt, fear, and pain. That night, he wallowed in dark emotions, which is something many unconsciously or consciously avoid doing, yet something necessary to do if we want to learn from the experience and grow into the best versions of ourselves. The simple universal truth reminded Bryant of the duality of life. Finding the light requires going through the darkness.

He tapped into the dark emotions of pain, ferocity, anger, and fear. After all, the night after the loss to Boston wasn't the first time he found inspiration in the darkest corners of his soul.

"Yeah, it's a scar, and it hurts...But if you manage to tap

into that pain and grow stronger from it, the sky is the limit." — Kobe on finding meaning in suffering

The next morning, any doubt was gone. In his own words, Kobe woke up and:
"It was back to business as usual."

Even if Bryant wanted to indulge in self-pity and misery, the new season was right around the corner. Kobe, the reigning NBA MVP, accepted the role in the USA squad for the upcoming summer Olympic games in Beijing, China. He was appointed as a team captain and the de-facto leader of the team dubbed 'The Redeem Team.'

The summer experience with the men's national team helped Bryant take his mind off the loss in the Finals.

He could focus on something larger than himself and larger than the Lakers' basketball. Now, he was on a mission to return the USA where it belongs, to the throne of the basketball world. *His experience with the national team and the Olympic games certainly broadened Kobe's leadership perspective.*

During the 2008 off-season, he started asking himself different kinds of questions. As any genuine leader, Kobe asked the first and the most difficult question:

"What happened, and what could I've done to prevent it?"

He realized Boston physically dominated the series, and he took ownership of that. Simply put, the Celtics were stronger and tougher when each game of the series was on the line. Years

later, reflecting back on this loss, Kobe simply stated:
'They beat the crap out of us.'

As a leader, Bryant considered it his duty to lead by example and to hold every teammate accountable for their actions. Looking back at the season behind, he realized he didn't challenge them enough, and more importantly, he didn't challenge them when it mattered the most.

Kobe took personal responsibility for that mistake. He held himself accountable, and sure enough, he never repeated it again.

> *"Leadership is often misconstrued....*
>
> *In 08, I finally understood that leadership is not about holding hands and singing Kumbaya with the rest of the guys. As a leader, you can't be afraid of confrontation if it means getting the best out of the team. As a leader, I will not be afraid of confrontation to get us to where we need to go.*
>
> *The simple truth is: If you are going to be a leader, you are not going to please everybody. You have to hold people accountable."– Kobe Bryant on his leadership evolution.*

The loss against the Celtics set Kobe on a much deeper path of self-discovery.
After the heartbreaking defeat, Kobe started questioning his ultimate dreams. He began re-evaluating his inner ideals, aspirations, and goals. Kobe's desire to be the greatest player of

all time was all the fire he ever needed to keep moving forward.

For as long as he could remember, he was chasing the standard of excellence set by the greatest player of all time, Michael Jordan. Kobe realized that the goal that fueled him all these years had changed. At the end of the day, people will still have different opinions on who is the greatest player of all time.

For some, the Greatest of all time was ***Magic Johnson*** or ***Larry Bird,*** the staples of basketball in the 80s. For many, many others, the best was ***Jordan***. ***Michael Jordan***, whose rise and domination coincided with the globalization of the game, certainly immortalized 'basketball greatness.'

For a new generation of basketball fans following the game in the early 2000s, the greatest ever was **Kobe**. For the even younger generation, the generation of today and tomorrow, the best might be **Lebron James**, **Steff Curry, or someone else entirely.**

The debate on the Greatest of all time will continue for as long as the game exists.

Bryant's inner ideal of greatness was now different. Kobe was on the quest to become the best version of himself. Now, Kobe's perspective shifted, and he asked himself a different question:

How can I be the greatest player that I can be?

Being the greatest player meant being the best leader he could possibly be. Suddenly, the game of basketball was so much more to him. Embracing the new challenge, he was on a quest to inspire greatness in his teammates.

With the realization, Kobe was ready to go to work.

He discovered the weak spots in his leadership and decided to do something about them. He learned that as an effective leader, he had to work on specific elements and character traits.

One of Kobe's greatest challenges was communicating effectively, as any leader should.

As much as he valued accountability as a trait in a teammate and wasn't afraid of confrontation, he discovered another value a true leader must possess — Empathy. The trick, as Kobe said, was in the balance of those things.

Genuine leadership is, first and foremost, about compassion. Once a genuine leader becomes aware of the notion, the next step has to be genuine listening to those around them.

Once Kobe started actually listening to his teammates, he discovered their unique life perspectives, and soon, he began getting to know who they really were. In turn, Kobe was willing to open up to the rest of the team. He started participating more in team activities and off-the-court bindings.

Magic Johnson, the Omni present figure in the Lakers franchise, noted the loss to the Celtics in '08 as a turning point for Kobe Bryant, the leader of the team. He said many times, and in various interviews, he saw a change in Bryant's leadership style after the defeat. Magic, who led the same dynasty throughout the '80s, believes Kobe's personality changed once he took the necessary loss.

Kobe started taking teammates to dinner, which was something inconceivable for the younger version of himself. This allowed him to connect with each and every one of the players on a personal level first. He understood their journeys. He realized what they were going through on a human level.

As a leader, Kobe realized every teammate responds differently, and for each teammate, he has to customize the approach for maximum results. With some players, he knew exactly how to strike the cord. *With others, he had to be patient, a virtue that Kobe tried to actively practice while leading the Los Angeles Lakers.*

> *"Passing the ball to an open teammate is a trivial way of looking at leadership. What you have to do is get them to want to be better. Get them to an emotional space where they wake up every morning eager to show up, compete and win.*
>
> *The trick is to get them to want to be the best version of themselves"*

Looking in the rearview mirror, the soul-crushing defeat against Boston was a blessing in disguise for Kobe. He needed the final lesson to truly understand what it takes to be great.

Being a great player is much more than being the best player of the generation today. Champions come and go. The best players of the generation come and go. Some are remembered and celebrated more than others.

To be truly great and remembered in history, you have to inspire greatness in those around you.

* * *

The Ultimate Leadership Test: Revenge Served With a Vengeance

Kobe took the lessons from the disappointing loss and worked on his leadership skills during the entire off-season, focusing on his communication skills while building team spirit and chemistry between players.

The change was evident. The next year, Kobe Bryant and the Lakers returned with a vengeance. From the opening game of the 2008–2009 season, it was crystal clear that the LA Lakers were on a mission.

They opened the campaign with seven straight wins.

Bryant led the team to tie the franchise record for most wins to start the season, going 17–2, and by the middle of December, they compiled a 21–3 record. Kobe was named Player of the Month for December and January. By the time mid-April rolled around and the playoffs began, the Lakers finished the regular season with the best record in the Western Conference (65–17).

Bryant was runner-up in the MVP voting behind *Lebron*

James, and he was selected to the All-NBA First Team and All-Defensive First Team for the seventh time in his career.

Despite marching through the regular season, Kobe and the rest of the team knew that there were no guarantees in the playoffs, and they had to guard against complacency.

Every single game had to be taken seriously. After all, LA had a similar situation just a year prior. They finished first in the western conference and easily ran through the opposition in the playoffs, beating *Denver Nuggets*, *Utah Jazz*, and *San Antonio Spurs* before losing to the Celtics in the playoffs finals.

Like the previous year, many predicted the rematch between LA and Boston in the grand finals. Unfortunately for all basketball fans around the globe, the Celtics shockingly lost to *Orlando Magic* in the Eastern Conference Semi-Finals.

On the route to the finals, LA fought and won against *Utah Jazz*, *Houston Rockets*, and *Denver Nuggets* before squaring off against the *Orlando Magic* in the playoffs finals. Despite the heroics Orlando managed to pull out to get to the finals, they were no match for Kobe and the LA Lakers.

Bryant dominated the finals, averaging 32.4 points, 5.6 rebounds, and 7.4 assists per game during the series, as LA won 4-1 to clinch their 15th title. Needless to say, Bryant won the Bill Russell NBA Finals MVP Trophy as he successfully led the team to the championship, proving all of the critics and naysayers wrong.

Kobe Bryant won his 4th championship, and he won his first one without Shaquille O'Neal. However, Kobe had no intention of stopping to rest on his laurels. He knew they had a winning formula, and he believed the Lakers could repeat the success the following year.

As a leader of the team, he wanted this generation of Los Angeles Lakers to be remembered by history as the back-to-back champions.

Although Kobe and the Lakers won the championship, they weren't truly tested on their road to success. Aside from the *Houston Rockets*, who extended the series to seven games purely by the power of their sheer will, no one else posed a real challenge for the Lakers.

The following season, the LA Lakers came out strong from the opening game, claiming their intention to defend the championship.

Throughout the entire league campaign, Kobe and the rest of the team dominated the league, finishing with a record of 57–25, which was enough to clinch the 1st spot in the heavily contested Western Conference. On their route to another NBA Finals, the Lakers won the first round against *Oklahoma City*, swept *Utah Jazz*, and steamrolled past *Phoenix Suns*.

On the other side of the playoff bracket, **over at the Eastern Conference, a familiar foe emerged.**

Despite the lackluster regular season, where they finished 4th in the Eastern Conference, the ***Boston Celtics*** consolidated at the right moment, just as the playoffs began. Much to the surprise of the entire basketball globe, Boston reached the NBA Finals,

and they scheduled another encounter with their arch-rival —
The Los Angeles Lakers.

Los Angeles was still haunted by the ghosts of the past.
Although the Lakers won the championship a year prior, Kobe
and the team haven't forgotten about the grueling physical se-
ries and the painful experience from two years prior. Although
Kobe had already lost one NBA Final in 04, the loss against the
Celtics loomed over his legacy.

Ever since he was a kid, he dreamt of being part of a historical
rivalry between LA and Boston, and he envisioned lifting a
trophy in the NBA finals against The Celtics. Kobe's worst fear
as a professional was to be remembered as part of the Lakers
who lost the finals to their mortal enemy. Making things harder
for Bryant was the fact that he wasn't a mere spectator or a role
player for the Lakers.

No.

He was the undisputed leader who failed to lead the team to
success and return the Lakers to their former glory. Despite all
the accolades and championships throughout his career, Kobe
dreamed of beating the Boston Celtics in the NBA finals.

In 2008, Kobe swore revenge.
Bryant admitted how much he wanted to win against Boston.
Many times, half-jokingly, he said he couldn't live with himself
knowing he was the leader of the Lakers, the generation who
lost twice to the Celtics in the NBA finals.

EVOLUTION & LEADERSHIP

He knew that they would meet Boston again simply because of the mere talent the Celtics possessed during those years. All-Star players such as *Paul Pierce, Kevin Garnett, Ray Allen,* and an emerging *Rajon Rondo*, backed up by proven veterans from the bench, were among the strongest superteams in the history of the NBA.

> *"Before the series with the Celtics, my challenge as a leader was to inspire the same ferocity in my team. The Celtics had to know they were not just playing against Kobe Bryant. They are playing against 12 people who are just like me, playing the game with the same intensity and focus."*
>
> *– Bryant on his approach to the 2010 NBA Finals.*

Just like two years before, the series was a physical matchup between two evenly matched-up teams. This time around, the Lakers responded adequately to the physical intensity of the Celtics. It was evident the Lakers wanted a payback. Full of confidence, the Los Angeles Lakers entered the finals.

Just like two years before, Boston focused all of its efforts on defending against Kobe, as that was the key to winning the last time. The strategy seemed to work according to the Celtics' plans. Boston took the lead in game five, making it a 3–2 lead in the best-of-seven series. They needed one more win in the next two games to clinch their record 18th NBA title.

With the **"Beat LA!"** chant reverberating in the famous **'TD Garden,'** Paul Pierce scored 27 points, and Kevin Garnett added

18 points with ten rebounds. In addition, Rajon Rondo had 18 points, eight assists, and five rebounds to help Boston become the first team in the series to win two games in a row.

If Los Angeles couldn't do the same at home, the Celtics would improve their record to 10–2 against the Lakers in the finals. Starting all the way from a 4–0 sweep over the Minneapolis Lakers in 1959 through the Bird-and-Magic era of the '80s and Boston's win in '08.

The pressure was on Kobe Bryant and the rest of the team, given the fact that The Celtics have never blown a 3–2 lead in the NBA finals. Interestingly, at the press conference after game 5 of the series, Kobe downplayed the importance of the rivalry. He said neither rivalry nor revenge should be motivating his teammates when they try to stave off elimination at home.

> *"Just man up and play. What the hell is a big deal? If I have to say something to them, then we don't deserve to be champions. We're down 3–2: Go home, win one game, and go into the next one. Simple as that."*
>
> *— Kobe at the press conference after the loss to the Celtics in game 5 of the 2010 NBA Finals*

By this point in his career, and after so many battles and wars he has been through, he was experienced enough to deflect the unnecessary pressure from his team.

Away from the cameras and reporters in the press room, Kobe's reaction was different. In the locker room, immediately after the defeat, the team was quiet and reflective. After all, the task ahead seemed almost impossible. Cool, calm, and collected, Kobe Bryant addressed the team in the locker room.

Years later, when asked what he said to his teammates after game five loss at the 'Garden,' Kobe shared a behind-the-scenes story.

"I remember entering the locker room and feeling the atmosphere. We were down 3–2, and they just demolished us. So, I looked at my teammates, and I started laughing. They all looked at me like I was insane and asked me: 'Why the hell are you laughing?!'

I told them:

"Look, they beat the crap out of us. That's ok because we still have two games to play in our home. If we win two games, we are the champions.

Think about it…

If someone came to you before the season and offered you this position right here, being down 3–2 before the final two games that we play at home, you would've taken the offer, right?

We have two more games, and we are taking it one game at a time. Let's win the first one, and I promise

**you, they are not going to win game seven on our
court. It's just not happening. ''**

The series returned to LA, and game 6 was anything but
competitive. The Lakers managed to grab an early lead, and
they stayed focused throughout the entire game. The end result
was a blowout win for the LA Lakers, and the series was tied at
3−3, meaning the entire season came down to the final game.

*Nine months of NBA basketball came down to the final three hours.
The grandest stage was set. The Los Angeles Lakers had a shot at
redemption.*

In game 7, The Celtics set the tone early by pushing the pace,
being physical, and playing lockdown defense on Kobe Bryant
— which was the proven recipe that brought them success in
08. By the end of the first quarter, the Lakers trailed by 9 points.
The Lakers were able to close the gap in the second quarter, but
they still went into halftime down by 6, and a big reason for
that was Bryant's shot selection.

With the heartbreaking result of the 2008 NBA Finals still fresh
in Bryant's mind, he tried to take over the game from the start,
forcing many bad shots in the first half.

Kobe's desire to get revenge was undeniable, but winning
required a different approach. Leading his team to another
championship required mid−game adjustment. Kobe made a
crucial observation midway through the second half. He found
a way of beating Boston. Kobe realized the path to victory was
simple: Rely on the team and trust your teammates.

Yet, as simple as it sounds, this was Bryant's ultimate leadership test:
Can you trust your teammates enough to rely on them in crucial moments?

Boston played phenomenal defense, which made Kobe struggle to score in the first half. Fortunately for the Lakers, like many times throughout the season, other players were ready to step up and contribute.

Coming out of halftime, the Lakers had an opportunity to force the Celtics to play at their pace, but they weren't successful, and Boston went on a 9–2 run to open the third quarter. Unexpectedly, starting point guard and a very important player for the Lakers, **Derek Fisher,** walked back to the locker room with an injury.

Right then and there, many Lakers fans started to relive the dreadful experience from 08, fearing the same scenario happening again.

With his legacy on the line, Bryant rallied his teammates in the fourth quarter. After all, he made a promise to his teammates that the Celtics would not win the series in the *Staples Center*, the heart of Los Angeles.

Instead of looking to score first, which is undoubtedly his first instinct, Kobe looked for a way to include and assist his teammates. The Celtics played tight and strict defense on him, leaving other players open.

They didn't expect Kobe to pass the ball in such critical moments.

Yet he did.

Although Kobe hit a few important shots, it was a collective effort that made all the difference. Pau Gasol, the same player who got the lion's share of the criticism after the 2008 NBA Finals, stepped up both offensively and defensively. In addition, Metta Sandiford-Artest (Formerly known as Ron Artest) hit the 3-point shot to give LA a 6-point lead with just a minute left on the clock.

On the other end of the floor, Boston couldn't deal with the Lakers' solid defense, failing to score the basket. With a few big shots from Fisher and World Peace and a tireless effort on the defensive end from Bryant, the Lakers managed to secure a narrow 83–79 victory over their arch-rival.

It took everything they had, but they did it — the Lakers beat the Celtics.

With this victory, Kobe won his fifth and final championship ring. Additionally, Bryant added another 'Finals MVP' to his resume. With tears in his eyes, Kobe lifted the NBA championship trophy high above his head as the team celebrated the success with the entire Laker nation in their home, *The Staples Center.*

For Kobe personally, this revenge had a deeper meaning.
With the victory in the 2010 NBA Finals, Kobe's leadership redemption arc concluded in the most satisfying manner - Fulfilling the

EVOLUTION & LEADERSHIP

childhood dream of beating The Celtics in the Finals.

8

Eternal Legacy: Greatness Echoes into Eternity

> *"I believe greatness is infinite growth. Every single day, you are getting better and better. Are you constantly growing?*
>
> *Greatness is not a destination; it's a process.*
>
> *If you have the mentality, then you'll continually chase greatness, and in the process, you'll realize that you'll never really achieve it....But you will keep getting better every single day. You'll continually strive to reach your fullest potential.*
>
> *I believe that process and that journey is greatness."*

In 2007, Kobe Bryant got an offer he couldn't refuse.

Mike Krzyzewski, the head coach of the US national team, called and asked Kobe to be a part of the ***"Redeem Team"*** scheduled to compete at the upcoming Olympics. Not only the coach needed Bryant on the team, but he also offered Kobe a captaincy role, making the expectations clear from the beginning. The USA needed Kobe Bryant to lead.

The clever wordplay the media used to dub the national team reveals a grim state of affairs and the immense pressure on the US team to bring back gold. Just four years prior, the USA was humiliated on the grand basketball stage when they only won the bronze medal at the previous Olympics in Athens, Greece.

The common goal of restoring former glory to the USA and winning back the respect of the entire world was more than enough to unite the selected NBA superstars. For the first time, Kobe Bryant felt a different kind of pressure. Kobe's responsibility was bigger than just winning with the Los Angeles Lakers and bigger than becoming the NBA Champion.

He felt his duty belonged to the entire country of America. Kobe Bryant accepted the challenge and joined the roster of NBA superstars already on the national team, players like *Lebron James, Dwayne Wade, Carmelo Anthony, Chris Paul, Dwight Howard,* and others.

In the typical Mamba fashion, he set the standard of excellence from the first day of practice in the training camp.
The wounds from the recent defeat in the NBA Finals were still fresh. The loss from the Celtics taught Kobe a valuable lesson. *He learned he had to lead by example.*

There was a loose ball within the first 30 seconds of the scrimmage, and Kobe dove head-first into the floor to get it. He did it over and over again, fighting for each possession and playing as intensely as if it were the Olympic Finals game. The message he sent from the first training was loud and clear:

The only way of redeeming the United States of America in the eyes of the basketball world was by winning. The only way of winning the gold medal was to go all in.

Up until that point in time, for all of his USA teammates, Kobe Bryant was an enigma. *Bill Plaschke*, a sports journalist who has written for the *Los Angeles Times* since 1987, reported on the 2008 Olympic Games premeeting and noted Kobe was sitting by himself.

Unlike other NBA players and superstars, Bryant never took the time to ingratiate himself with the other players in the league. The man once famously said: *"I don't take a vacation just for the sake of a vacation. I see many other players take a vacation together and go fishing or just chill. I could never do that."*

Although wary at first, his US teammates saw the desire and soon followed his lead, trying their best to match his intensity. He brought the best out of the NBA superstars, and he brought their competitive spirit to the surface. They knew Kobe as they played against him in the NBA, and they knew he was a fierce competitor.

Nevertheless, they were oblivious to his training methods and his approach to the game of basketball. After all, this was the first time they were exposed to **The Mamba Mentality** outside their common battleground.

However, it was the same Mamba Mentality that bonded the group.

Dwyane Wade recounted a story of the Mamba Mentality to ESPN's Michael Wallace about the 2008 Olympics.

> *"We're in Las Vegas, and we all come down for team breakfast at the start of the whole training camp, And Kobe comes in with ice on his knees and with his trainers and stuff.*
>
> *He's got sweat drenched through his workout gear. I remember thinking: 'It's 8 o'clock in the morning, man. Where in the hell is he coming from?*
>
> *Everybody else just woke up... We're all yawning, and he's already three hours and a full workout into his day."*
>
> — *Dwayne Wade on Kobe's standard of greatness*

The domino effect was inevitable, and it was immediate.
Within a few days, Kobe got company for his 5 AM workouts. The first to follow the lead were *Lebron James* and *Dwayne Wade*. By the rest of the week, the entire USA national team was on Kobe's schedule, practicing together before sunrise.

After the training camp in Vegas, Kobe had fully accessed the situation. He had a clear picture of the team and what he needed to do for the US to win the Olympics. Bryant realized the path to victory was through personal sacrifice. The sacrifice that started with him.

Sacrificing for the cause meant sacrificing personal stats on the offensive end of the game. Kobe knew that each and every player on the US team could score on any given night against any given opponent. Their weakness lay elsewhere.

What Bryant did next shocked the coach, Mike Krzyzewski. Before the Olympic tournament in Beijing started, he came to the coach's office with a specific request. **He asked Krzyzewski to put him in charge of the defense**. Naturally, Kobe would always score points, but his focus would be on stopping the opposing team's best scorer. He made a promise he would destroy whoever that best scorer was.

Coach Krzyzewski agreed. Throughout his entire coaching history, Kobe Bryant was the first player who ever came to him pleading to focus on the defense. Yet, Bryant wasn't like any other player. The only thing that mattered was winning, and he was willing to do anything he could for the sake of that mission.

The man once called a 'Selfish Showboat' and a man revered for his acrobatics, flashy moves, and lethal scoring has certainly come a long way.

He was the driving force behind restoring US basketball back to its former glory, the place where it belongs. The United States of America ran through the tournament, demolishing the opponents. During the entire Olympics, their game was a symphony, with each superstar contributing in various ways and at different stages of the game. The redemption journey concluded triumphantly after the Olympic Finals game, where they beat *Spain*. The USA won the long-awaited gold medal.

Kobe's experience with the US national basketball team at the Olympics broadened his horizons. The game of basketball became larger than just himself.

He still felt the same drive deep within him, but he found new meaning in the game of basketball.

Give Back and Inspire the Next Generation

> "Some people become great and don't give back, but Kobe was giving back to the next generation. He trained boys and girls, pros or middle school athletes. He wanted to pass his knowledge along to people to bring the game to new heights."
> — Carlos Boozer, 2008 US Olympic Teammate.

The final stage of Kobe's basketball evolution came around 2013. By this point, he had established himself as one of the most accomplished players in the history of the game, one of the All-Time Greats, and a man who was well on the way to transcend the game of basketball.

In fact, since 2013, once revered fearless competitor looking to 'kill' and humiliate any opponent, Kobe embraced a new role. He became a mentor and a teacher to younger NBA talents.

Kobe understood the nature of the game is to evolve. He believed the nature of basketball reflects the nature of life itself, and he did his best to pass on the knowledge, wisdom, and inspiration to the next generation.

Growing up, Bryant believed in the undeniable power of the Muse.

Originating from ancient Greek religion and mythology, the *Muses* are the inspirational goddesses of literature, science, and the arts. They were considered the source of the knowledge embodied in the poetry, lyric songs, and myths that were related orally for centuries in ancient Greek culture. In modern figurative usage, a Muse may be a source of artistic inspiration.

As an avid reader of classic literature and history, early on in his life, Kobe discovered the notion of the Muse, and he would apply it to all of his endeavors in life, starting with basketball.

Kobe Bryant was inspired by many great players on his basketball journey, yet his basketball Muses, those he learned the most from, were ***Jerry West, Magic Johnson, and Michael Jordan.*** Kobe was inspired by their level of mastery of the craft, and he aspired to reach their unprecedented heights of basketball greatness.

Because these greats raised the bar of excellence, Kobe Bryant had an ideal to strive for. Kobe dedicated himself to the journey of greatness, and throughout his entire career, these three legends of the game provided nothing but guidance and support.

Just as his muses once did with him, Bryant inspired, guided, and mentored the greatest players of today, such as **Lebron James, Dwayne Wade, Carmello Anthony, Steph Curry, Kyrie Irving, Luka Doncic, Jayson Tatum, Giannis Antetokounmpo**, and many other superstars.

Since his retirement, Kobe was still involved with basketball as he found other ways of giving back to the game he loved. It turned out his daughter **Gianna** had the same **Mamba Mentality.** Just as competitive, just as driven to win, and sharing the same joy towards the game of basketball.

More than 30 years ago, Kobe Bryant fell in love with the game by watching his father do what he does best. Just like Joe Bryant inspired love for basketball in young Kobe, life came full circle for the Bryants when Gianna, who was still a toddler, began accompanying him to the practices and games.

Mesmerized by her father playing basketball, the little girl would sit on the bench and be amazed by the game unfolding in front of her. As she got a bit older, her love for the game was clear as a day, and her desire to be the best was undeniable. There were no uncertainties or doubts about her future.

She discovered a gift deep within her, much like her father did once upon a time - The gift of pure and unconditional love for the game of basketball. There was nothing in the world she'd rather do than play. Her character, on the other hand, wanted to compete and win. *Gianna was committed to her life purpose — to be the greatest player in the WNBA.*

Kobe was inspired by her love and devotion to the craft, and in 2018, he founded ***Mamba Sports Academy*** — a State-of-the-art training and performance institute with a single mission in mind: **Help, train, and guide young athletes to become the best version of themselves.**

> *"MAMBA Sports Academy is a natural expansion of my commitment to educating and empowering the next generation of kids through sports."*
>
> *— Kobe Bryant's press release after establishing the Mamba Sports Academy*

As usual, Kobe entered into a new venture well-prepared. He did his homework, and he partnered with top professionals and experts from the health and fitness sphere. Together with his business partner *Chad Faulkner,* Bryant opened the Mamba Sports Academy in Thousand Oaks, California. In less than a year, the facility became Mecca for elite young athletes from all over the world, supporting more than 50,000 students annually.

During the off-season in the summer, Kobe held basketball clinics and seminars in his academy for players with various levels of professional competence. For those in the NBA, the seminars were invitation only, and those who wished to participate had to commit to being fully present throughout the duration of the clinic.

Regular attendees were players like *Kyrie Irving, Paul George, and Kawhi Lenard.* In video footage circulating on the internet, Kobe shows his students certain moves in the post, specifically a step-through layup and his signature mid-range fadeaway shot. The trick, as **The Master of The Fundamentals** explained to his students, wasn't in a move but the **footwork behind it.**

> *"The most important thing for players that come after me is to never limit your imagination because people may think you are crazy.... But if we as athletes don't think it's possible to achieve greatness, then how are we going to inspire the next generation to do the same?"*

The great testament to Kobe's influence on the game of basketball came when Kawhi Lenard made the statement on the grandest stage of them all.

During his famous playoff run in 2019, when he led the Toronto Raptors to their first-ever championship, Lenard's playing style and almost God-like performance drew many comparisons with Kobe Bryant. The shades of **The Mamba Mentality** in Kawhi's game were obvious to any basketball fan as he danced on the court, relying on his mid-range pull-up shot and fadeaway jumper, which he perfected after working with the legend.

Kobe's impact on the game of basketball goes way beyond men's basketball.

Kobe Bryant was a champion and an advocate for women's basketball rights, and his support for women's basketball extended to the college level. He and Gianna became close friends with University of Oregon star *Sabrina Ionescu*, regularly attending her games. Kobe even dedicated an episode of his ESPN+ show 'Detail' to analyzing Sabrina's game.

Kobe's greatest joy post-retirement was coaching Gianna's middle school girl's basketball team. About six months after retiring from the NBA, he started coaching the Mamba Sports Academy girl's middle school basketball team.

Through coaching Gianna and her teammates, Kobe taught the girls the value of hard work, dedication, and, most importantly, the value of having fun playing basketball.

Speaking with Frank Buckley from KTLA5 in 2019, Kobe Bryant revealed his philosophy and approach to coaching and teaching the game of basketball.

> *"You get better incrementally. Everybody's standard of excellence is different. The most important thing is that you become the best version of yourself. That is the key.*
>
> *Get better every single day.*
>
> *Are you better today than you were yesterday? If the answer is yes, you are on the right track. That's The Mamba Mentality."*

* * *

Beyond The Horizon: The Journey To Infinity

Kobe took the lessons from basketball and applied them to his new ventures. Aside from running on full steam with the Mamba Sports Academy, he was involved with various other passion projects. Since retiring from the game, Kobe has maintained his intensity and worked as hard as ever.

The list of his accomplishments after retiring is both admirable and perplexing. Since retiring from the game of basketball, Kobe Bryant:

- Founded Granity Studios
- Released Two Films: The Muse for Showtime and Dear Basketball
- Won an Emmy and an Oscar award for Dear Basketball
- Wrote and published a book, The Mamba Mentality: How I play
- Wrote, produced, and published the 'Wizenard' Series of books
- Served as a producer and host of 'Detail: Breaking Down Basketball Series' and 'Musecage' for ESPN
- Created a podcast series, 'The Punnies'
- The most significant accomplishment for Kobe Bryant was co-creating his fourth baby girl. Vanessa and Kobe welcomed *Capri Bryant* to this world in June 2019.

In the last chapter of his story, Kobe Bryant was inspired to reach limits grander than infinity. His intention was reflected in the name of his content production company — 'Granity Studios.' In a typical Mamba Fashion, he put the two words together and created a new word. With it, he gave new meaning to greatness.

Kobe Bryant was a man with a vision, and he was very much looking to the future.

Although he knew perfection was impossible, he strived for it with the same enthusiasm and passion. **In all of his endeavors, Kobe Bryant was driven by a singular purpose:**

Give back and Inspire the next generation.

Unfortunately, he didn't get to realize his dreams and goals. It feels like Kobe was taken too soon from life, as there were so many great things still on the horizon. The curse of being a human is that we often don't get to understand the Divine reasons.

On the other hand, the miracle of our existence is that we get to experience Life in all of its glory. We get to witness a story of someone else's greatness, inspiring us to embark on our own unique journey.

Every once in a while, someone like Kobe Bryant comes around, reminding us of our inherent greatness and showing us the full magnificence of the human spirit.

Like very few before or after him, Kobe Bryant made a dent in the universe.
His time on Earth was cut short, but his impact and legacy will live on in eternity. He lived a fulfilling life full of meaningful experiences and moments. Just like he was teaching the game of basketball to the next generation, Kobe's priceless lessons and wisdom could teach us a lot about life.

For those pursuing success clues in the story of Kobe Bryant, look no further than how the man lived his life. Kobe's life philosophy and approach to basketball are forever encapsulated and immortalized in the form of **The Mamba Mentality.** The way he lived his life with *The Mamba Mentality* serves as a testament to his desire to reach greatness, which lies beyond infinity.

Kobe's ultimate legacy is the people whose lives he touched, those he inspired to be better, and all of us he inspired on our journey to becoming our best selves.

> *"You have to dance beautifully in the box that you're comfortable dancing in. My box was to be extremely ambitious within the sport of basketball.*
>
> *Your box is different than mine. Everybody has their own.*
>
> *It's your job to try to perfect it and make it as beautiful of a canvas as you can make it. And if you have done that, then you have lived a successful life. You have lived with Mamba Mentality."*

* * *

A personal note from the author:

In case you've enjoyed your experience with this book, please consider leaving a short review and a rating. In case a short written review is too much to ask, you can simply rate the experience you feel describes your satisfaction with this book.

Log in to Amazon, click on 'Your account,' and then click on

'Orders.' From your history of purchases, select this book and leave your rating.

It will take less than 60 seconds to complete. On the other hand, for an independent writer and publisher, your review and rating mean the world to me. My dream is to reach a million readers, and every single rating and positive review brings me one step closer to that dream.

Regardless of your choice, I want to thank you from the bottom of my heart. Thank you for getting a copy of this book, and thank you for the time we spent on this journey.

I hope you've learned something new, Gained an Insight, or received a Nugget of Wisdom.

Until next time,

Alex Karadzin

About the Author

From one reader to another – I'd like to welcome you to the most exclusive arbitrary 'Cover to Cover Book Club!' I appreciate you for taking a few moments to get to know me.

My name is Alex Karadzin, a proud Serbian born in beautiful Bosnia in a great country once known as Yugoslavia.

I am a multimedia artist, an author, a lifelong student, and a modern-day teacher.

Ever since I was a child, I was encouraged by my family to explore as far as the outer limits of my mind go. My curious attitude toward life and my wondrous spirit led me to many unusual places.

One of them was the nightlife industry.

For about three years, I was a nightlife photographer, living the rock and roll lifestyle to the fullest. Through my nightlife job and this social environment, I have learned so much about human psychology and social dynamics, but most of all, I learned so much about myself.

Aside from photography, I am an amateur actor and athlete.

My other interests and passions include philosophy, spirituality, history, fitness, and mixed martial arts. I have various hobbies that mostly include some aspects of self-development rituals in them.

I am an avid content consumer and a voracious reader. Life-long learning is deeply ingrained into the very essence of my being.

Knowing "Who I am" is my North Star for what I do professionally.

I work as a Learning and Transformational Designer. My job is to create a framework for the learning experience that takes place in the physical or digital world.

Physically in the form of: Seminars and training, various types of conferences, and live events. In an online format, I do most of my work as an online content and course creator, mostly in the domain of personal development.

I have been part of the personal development industry for the last eight years, working in one of the biggest companies in the world, Mindvalley.

In 2018, I decided to follow my heart and soul and leave Malaysia to work on my personal projects and ventures. One of them was the *Connection Rockstar* Platform.

I had a vision of bringing brilliant people together to learn and, eventually, teach others by sharing their knowledge.

ABOUT THE AUTHOR

The content on the platform was primarily about social dynamics, human psychology, and behavior. Over time, I have experimented with different content formats and different content consumer experiences.

In a hardly explainable serendipity moment, I ended up in the publishing industry in late 2020.

As an author and independent publisher, I have produced a diverse range of books on topics including personal growth and self-help, charisma, communication, and social skills. In addition to producing books under my own name, I have ghost-written books in a variety of niches, including children's non-fiction and fiction, trivia and fun facts, health and wellness, history, short fiction, and short non-fiction stories.

The most rewarding accomplishment from my publishing endeavor has to be the success of my best-selling series *"How To Win The Game of Life: Success Leaves Clues."*

So far the edition has found its readers on six continents and 20+ countries.

These books are designed for a comprehensive, immersive learning and transformative experience for the reader. This edition is carefully crafted and intended for those who are wholeheartedly committed to life-long learning and unlocking their fullest potential.

As of 2023, I am still on a never-ending quest to challenge the status quo as I expand the limits of my perception, searching for answers and the wisdom that comes with those answers.

As I go along my journey, I want to share that wisdom, serve, and encourage others to be Rockstars and live their life to the fullest. I believe in the idea that everybody can live a meaningful life on their own terms.

Life is about freedom, expression, experiences, people, and ultimately...contribution.

The Quote I live by:

> **"Your life is not about you. Your life is about everyone else whose life you touch and the way in which you do so."** — **Neale Donald Walsch**

Also by Alex Karadzin

"Success Leaves Clues" is a series with only one goal - Deconstructing highly successful individuals and their success models.

What is it that high achievers do differently?

What are their beliefs, rituals, and habits that made them reach the top of the mountain?

Most importantly, what success lessons can we take from them and apply in our own lives?

"Success Leaves Clues" is a series of action-oriented manuals that offers a **psychoanalytical breakdown and behavioral model for success.**

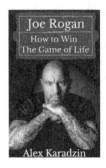

Joe Rogan: How to Win the Game of Life: Success, Habits, Mindset and Life Lessons How to Win The Game of Life?

Joe Rogan is a trailblazer and a trendsetter who shaped the cultural landscape we live in. The man who defied the odds at every step of his journey, Joe is one of the most influential personalities of today. His journey and unusual outlook on life took him to the top of the world.

This modern-day renaissance man shows us how to win in the game of life.

In this success guide, we will take a deeper look at the life of Joe Rogan and deconstruct his powerful success models.

This guidebook is designed as a learning experience for the reader. In it, we'll cover the following aspects of Joe Rogan's unique personality and success:

1. Joe Rogan Origin Story
2. Modern-Day Renaissance Man
3. Raw Authenticity
4. World-Class Discipline & Work Ethic
5. Charisma

Additionally, there is a breakdown of each chapter and a concrete 'How To' aspect you can model and replicate in your everyday life.

This guidebook is not for you if:
You expect to find facts and a list of accomplishments. Dry facts about Joe Rogan's life and career are available elsewhere.

This guidebook is for you if:
You are a true fan of Joe Rogan.

You are into personal development and you want to see a detailed breakdown of Joe Rogan's success mindset, habits, and life lessons.

Exclusive from the "Success Leaves Clues" series.

Zlatan Ibrahimović: The Way of The Outsider: Life Lessons in Success
From the Ghetto Streets to The Hotel Suites, Zlatan Ibrahimovic has Cracked The Code to Success.

Zlatan is a success outlier, an underdog who rose above all the challenges and obstacles life threw at him. Zlatan Ibrahimovic came a long way from delinquent stealing bicycles in Rosengard to the absolute pinnacle of a multi-billion-dollar football industry.

How did Zlatan defy expectations and break the mold of society?

In this success guide, we will take a deeper look at the life of Zlatan Ibrahimovic and deconstruct his powerful success models.

Through the retrospect of Zlatan's life and career, we shine the light on specific points from his illustrious career. We will relive some of the most glorious moments of Zlatan's career, the highs and lows of his life, and lessons in success.

In the latest edition of the "Success Leaves Clues Series," we will explore the intriguing mind and the complex character of Zlatan Ibrahimovic — one of the most controversial personalities in the history of sports.

Zlatan Ibrahimovic: The Way of The Outsider

In this success case study, you'll find **Zlatan's psychoanalytical breakdown and his behavioral model for success.** Through

Zlatan's personal stories and well-known moments in time and history, we'll explore and focus on the following:

1. Origin Story

2. Bulletproof Confidence

3. Who Are You? (The Role of Identity and Self-Image)

4. Charisma

5. Success Mindset & Character of a Champion

6. The Final Piece of Zlatan's Success Puzzle

This guidebook is not for you if:
You expect to find facts and a list of accomplishments. Dry facts about Zlatan's life and career are available elsewhere. (Try Wikipedia)

This guidebook is for you if:
1. You are a true fan of Zlatan Ibrahimovic. You want to get to know Zlatan from a slightly different perspective, from a viewpoint that you haven't seen before.

2. You are a genuine Football Fan. (Soccer Fan)

3. You are into personal development, and you want to see a detailed **breakdown of Zlatan Ibrahimovic's success mindset, character & personality, and lessons in success.**

4. You are looking for a perfect gift for your loved one, a fan of Zlatan Ibrahimovic.

Exclusive from the "Success Leaves Clues" series.

How To Win The Game of Life: Dwayne Johnson: The Rock's Tactical Masterclass in Taking Over Hollywood & Dominating the World

How to Win The Game of Life?

In an age of social media influencers and internet celebrities, Dwayne Johnson's star shines the brightest. The Rock is a trendsetter with the Midas touch—everything he touches turns to gold. Dwayne, a former professional wrestling superstar and trailblazer at this core, achieved something no one else dared to try.

The Rock laid the Smackdown on the most ruthless industry and made Hollywood conform to him.

With a strategic decade-long plan, he set in motion a series of events that led to his rise to the top of the mountain in the entertainment and showbiz industry. Dwayne 'The Rock' Johnson became a universally beloved global icon, transcending borders and cultures. With his brilliant career strategy and business endeavors, The Rock has become a full-blown enterprise worth $800 million.

In other words, Dwayne Johnson has reached his destination — the intersection of greatness and global impact. The man with an impeccable reputation, Dwayne is a winner and leader with a proven track record of success. His journey to greatness is a testament to the innate power of the human spirit. The Rock's story of hardships and triumph serves as a beacon of inspiration for millions around the world.

The craziest part of his journey?

More than a decade ago, he was at rock bottom. Broken, alone, and depressed, Dwayne was in a dire situation. His stock price was at an all-time low, and his star power was in jeopardy of fading to obscurity. Disappearing from mainstream consciousness was a real possibility for a once-promising talent. His movie career was hanging by a thread as the industry rapidly changed, and Hollywood slammed every door in his face.

With the cultural shift on the horizon, The Rock saw an opportunity to seize his dreams and win the game of life. With his back against the wall, The Rock made his last stand and resorted to one final move. Together with his dedicated team, Dwayne Johnson devised a strategic playbook — a tactical masterclass in success — for a hostile takeover and global domination.

The million-dollar question almost imposes itself:
What's in it for you, and why should you get your hands on The Rock's tactical masterclass on winning the game of life?

The book's central theme is Dwayne Johnson's Hollywood takeover and his rise to becoming a global icon. Each chapter follows his journey, and each story covers a specific period in his life. We will stroll down memory lane and pinpoint moments in time that defined The Rock and forged him into the powerhouse we all know and love today. Expect a deep dive into Dwayne's foundational values, success principles, and life philosophies, which he used to conquer the worlds of professional wrestling, cinema, and business.

Yet, this book's 'North Star' is to provide you with insights, strategies, and tactics to reclaim your innate power and win the game of life. At the end of each chapter, we will break down the underlying principles and methods The Rock used to achieve his vision. In the 'How to' section of each chapter, you will receive a step-by-step guide for applying these principles in your life for maximum success results.

"*How to Win The Game of Life: Success Leaves Clues*" edition is the only book series on the market that teaches you the hidden and untold secrets of the Greats. This series differs from any other, as these books are designed for a comprehensive, immersive learning and transformative experience. It is intended for those who are wholeheartedly committed to life-long learning, unlocking their fullest potential, and living their greatest lives.

If you are ready to discover Dwayne Johnson's untold strategy for Winning The Game of Life - Order your copy now!

Printed in Great Britain
by Amazon